Blackstone's
ANNUAL UPDATE
1990

FAMILY LAW

Barbara Mitchels LLB, Solicitor

BLACKSTONE
PRESS LIMITED

First published in Great Britain 1990 by Blackstone Press Limited,
9–15 Aldine Street, London W12 8AW. Telephone 01-740 1173

© B. Mitchels, 1990

ISBN: 1 85431 084 4

British Library Cataloguing in Publication Data
A CIP catalogue record for this book is available from the British Library

Typeset and printed by Precise Printing & Communications Ltd, Leatherhead, Surrey

All rights reserved. No part of this book may be reproduced or transmitted in any form or by any means, electronic or mechanical, including photocopying, recording, or any information storage or retrieval system without prior permission from the publisher.

CONTENTS

	Preface...	vii
1	**Statutes**...	1
	Children Act 1989.................................	1
2	**Statutory Instruments**...........................	28
	Legal Aid in Criminal and Care Proceedings (Costs) Regulations 1989..................................	28
	Legal Aid in Criminal and Care Proceedings (General) Regulations 1989..................................	33
	Blood Tests (Evidence of Paternity) (Amendment) Regulations 1989..................................	37
	Child Abduction and Custody (Parties to Conventions) (Amendment) (No. 2) Order 1989	38
	Child Abduction and Custody (Parties to Conventions) (Amendment) (No. 3) Order 1989	38
	Matrimonial Causes (Costs) (Amendment) Rules 1989	38
	Matrimonial Causes (Costs) (Amendment No. 2) Rules 1989	41
	Children and Young Persons (Amendment) Act 1986 (Commencement No. 2) Order 1988	41
	Accommodation of Children (Charge and Control) Regulations 1988..................................	41
	Boarding Out of Children (Foster Placement) Regulations 1988..................................	42
	Magistrates' Courts (Custodianship Orders) (Amendment) Rules 1989	44
	Family Law Reform Act 1987 (Commencement No. 2) Order 1989.......................................	45
	Legal Aid Act 1988 (Commencement No. 3) Order 1989	48
	Access to Personal Files (Social Services) Regulations 1989	49

3	**Cases**	51
	Brewer v Brewer	51
	R v North Yorkshire County Council, *ex parte* M	52
	Re G	54
	Re W (A Minor)	56
	Sadiq v Chief Adjudication Officer	57
	Re P (A Minor)	58
	Re C (A Minor)	60
	R v Lancashire County Council, *ex parte* Moore (A Minor)	62
	Waterman v Waterman	64
	Attorney-General's Reference (No. 1 of 1989)	66
	B v T	68
4	**Circulars and Official Publications**	71
	Home Office Circular 24/1989	71
	The Children Act 1989 Notice of Royal Assent and of the Provisions to Take Early Effect	73
	Introduction to the Children Act 1989	75
5	**Commercial Publications**	76
	Representing Children: Child Interviews – A Pictorial Aid for Guardians *ad Litem* and Child Care Panel Solicitors by D. Clark	76
	Law and the Family by John Dewar	76
	Mothers without Custody by G. Grief and M. Pabst ...	78
	Adoption Act Manual by Richard Jones	79
	Legal Issues in Human Reproduction edited by Sheila McLean	79
	Electronically Recorded Evidence: A Guide to the Use of Tape and Video Recordings in Criminal and Civil Proceedings by Sybil Sharpe	80
	Child Care and the Courts by C.R. Smith, M.T. Lane and T. Walsh	80
	Focus on Child Abuse edited by A. Levy	81
	Divorce, Legal Procedures and Financial Facts edited by Edith Rudinger	81
	Distribution of Matrimonial Assets on Divorce by Michael L. Rakusen, Dr Peter Hunt and A. Jane Bridge	82

Blackstone's
ANNUAL UPDATE
1990

FAMILY LAW

PREFACE

1989 has brought many changes in the field of family law. The movement for radical reform of child law arose originally, perhaps, from the publicity concerning the sad death of Maria Colwell in 1969, followed by the deaths of Jasmine Beckford, Kimberly Carlile and Tyra Henry. It was abundantly clear that the existing law inadequately protected children at risk.

The result is the Children Act 1989 (referred to in the text below as 'the Act') – described by the Lord Chancellor as 'The most comprehensive and far-reaching reform of child care law . . . in living memory' – which received royal assent on 16 November 1989. A few provisions of the Act have been brought into force straight away and it is proposed that the Act will be fully in effect by October 1991.

The Act was debated at length in Parliament, with over four hundred amendments being considered during its various stages. It went through quite a few radical changes during its journey through Parliament, and further innovative measures, including the child assessment order recommended by the NSPCC and the Association of Directors of Social Services, were added in as amendments.

The Children Act 1989 reflects a shift in attitude in that where a parent chooses to place a child in the care of a local authority it is now seen as a way of trying to keep the family together in the longer term, rather than a failure on the part of the parent. There is emphasis on local authority support for the family, and an underlying assumption that parents will have contact with their children unless this is not in the child's best interests. Parents will be encouraged to take part in decision making about their child, and access to children in care will be controlled by the court, no longer resting entirely in the discretion of the local authority.

The Act contains the first step towards the creation of a family court, despite comments in the Bill's early stages that this was not yet intended to happen because of a lack of human and financial resources. The Act creates 'the court' comprising the magistrates' court, the county court and the High Court. The various powers created in the Act are given to 'the court' with the intention that cases should be commenced in one of the levels within the court and then moved around as necessary within the hierarchy.

As the Act is implemented it will repeal a considerable amount of former legislation, including some of the sections of the Family Law Reform Act 1987 only recently brought into force. Practitioners will have to watch carefully for these changes as implementation of the Act takes place and (in addition to reading the update series!) notice each relevant announcement as it is made.

More detail of the Act follows in the text below at page 1. Until the full implementation of the Act, practitioners will have to work with the old law and parts of the new legislation. This will inevitably lead to complications for both practitioners and the courts, not to mention clients. The Act makes transitional provisions, and these will have to be studied carefully.

However, it is not only the Children Act 1989 which has occupied Parliament this year. The Legal Aid Act 1988 came into force in April 1989. Whilst not itself wildly innovative, taken with comments recently made by the Lord Chancellor, it looks as though very soon, fixed fees, already established in the Crown Court, will be introduced for magistrates' court cases.

Affiliation proceedings have gone. The Family Law Reform Act 1987 is now mainly in force, and as a result all applications for financial relief in respect of illegitimate children will now take place under the Guardianship of Minors Act 1971. Putative fathers may apply for parental rights, sharing these with the mother, or with a guardian. They will now be able to give or withhold consent to adoption, and become a party to care proceedings.

Last, but not least, is the Access to Pesonal Files Act 1987, in force since April 1989, giving people a right to see the personal information held about them by the Department of Social Services. On written request and payment of a fee, the local authority must provide access to specified information. There are, of course, careful safeguards; and access may not be given to information about others.

There have been many interesting and useful cases this year and selection has been difficult. As to the future, adoption law is under

PREFACE

review; there are developments anticipated in conciliation services; and soon there will be arrangements to be made prior to implementation of the Act including further training for magistrates and judiciary.

All in all, 1989 was quite a year!

Barbara Mitchels
December 1989

1

STATUTES

Children Act 1989

General comment
Most practitioners in the field of child care and family law will by now be aware of 'the most comprehensive and far-reaching reform of child care law . . . in living memory' (to quote the Lord Chancellor). He was referring, of course, to the Children Act 1989, referred to below as 'the Act'. On 16 November 1989, it received Royal Assent, and it will be implemented in stages, becoming wholly in force by October 1991. Mr David Mellor, Minister for Health, confirmed during the consideration of the Bill in Parliament on 23 October 1989 that it is a major consolidation and reform of both the private and public law relating to children; that it had proceeded through both houses of Parliament as a non-partisan measure; and that the government had offered a number of concessions to the opinions of all parties, meaning that a number of the amendments reflect agreements which were reached in committee. Parliament, amazingly, dealt with the 447 amendments very quickly. Drafting the Act proved to be even more complex, perhaps, than first envisaged.

Reform was certainly much needed. Child law was a tangled mass, difficult to find, let alone understand, and, being inconsistent, hard to apply. Another problem was that one had to work out which type of proceedings, in which court, could provide the required remedy before commencing action. This problem is solved by the Act which creates 'the court', defined in s.92(7) as 'the High Court, a county court or a magistrates' court'. The Lord Chancellor may make rules requiring specified classes of proceedings to be commenced only in certain courts; or limit jurisdiction in relation to specified proceedings, or the transfer of cases from one court to another. Application may be made under the Act to 'the court' for whatever order is required (subject to some exceptions, e.g. financial orders), and the only question of jurisdiction for consideration is at which level in the court to commence the proceedings or make subsequent transfers. Appeal from a magistrates' court decision under the Act will now lie to the High Court.

The Act reforms and consolidates much of the private law relating to children, wholly repealing nine previous statutes, and breaking new ground in many ways. For clarity, there follows a discussion of the main provisions of the Act following the order of the Act itself.

The Act is set out in 12 parts and has 15 schedules.

Part I
General principles. The Act embodies, in s.1, the general principle applicable where the court determines any question with respect to the upbringing of a child, the administration of a child's property or the application of any income arising from it; namely that the child's welfare shall be the paramount consideration for the court. This is already the overriding principle in wardship, but now it is firmly embodied in the Act and will apply in the magistrates' court, the county court and the High Court. Section 1(2) adds the further principle that any delay in determining the question is likely to prejudice the welfare of the child. Note that the principles outlined above do not appear to apply to the consideration of ancillary financial relief, nor to other matters unrelated to the child's upbringing.

When the court is deciding whether to make, vary or discharge an order under s.8 of the Act, or is considering care or supervision under Part IV of the Act, it must have regard to certain considerations set out in s.1(3), which include the wishes and feelings of the child; physical, emotional and educational needs; age, sex and background; harm which has been suffered or which he is at risk of suffering; his parents' ability to meet his needs; and the range of powers available under the Act in the proceedings in question.

Parental responsibility. 'Parental responsibility' is defined in s.3(1) as 'all the rights, duties, powers, responsibilities and authority which by law a parent of a child has in relation to the child and his property'. This concept does not entail the same rights as a former custody order, but it enables the person with parental responsibility to make some decisions in the child's life.

Parental responsibility will automatically lie with both the mother and father of a child if married to each other at the time of birth (or conception), but if the mother is unmarried, she alone has parental responsibility unless the natural father acquires it under the Act (s.2(1) and (2)). Parental responsibility is extended by s.3(2) to include the rights of a guardian appointed before the commencement of s.5 (which makes new provisions for the appointment of guardians, see below).

Parental responsibility can be acquired by agreement or court order (s.4); and more than one person may have parental responsibility at the same time (s.2(5)).

It would be very difficult for a person with whom a child lives (who does not already have parental responsibility, i.e., not being a parent or guardian) to manage without having parental responsibility for the child and so, under s.12(2), the court has power to give parental responsibility to a person in whose favour it makes a residence order under s.8 of the Act. Such a person will not, however, be able to consent to adoption or appoint a guardian for the child (s.12(3)). If the residence order is later discharged for any reason, that person may be able to retain his or her parental responsibility.

Guardianship changes. A guardian may now only be appointed under the provisions of the Act. The Guardianship of Minors Act 1971 and the Guardianship Act 1973 will be wholly repealed. The provisions relating to guardianship are all in ss.5 and 6 of the Act.

A person with parental responsibility may appoint a guardian to take over those responsibilities when he or she dies (s.5(3)). Similarly, a guardian may appoint another to replace him on his death (s.5(4)). Appointments may be made only in the way set out in the Act in s.5(5), i.e., in writing, signed and dated. Attestation by two witnesses of the execution by another of the appointment (in the presence of the witnesses) is required where the appointer is unable to sign the appointment personally. Although these provisions are similar to those for a will, they are less strict, and the Act sets out to render appointments fairly informal, perhaps to encourage the appointment of guardians. Appointments in a will or codicil are still valid, and subject to provisions of the Wills Act 1837.

In certain situations, the court may step in to appoint a guardian of a child, where there is no parent with parental responsibility for the child; or where a parent or guardian dies whilst a residence order in his or her favour is in force, (s.5(1)). Such an order may be made of the court's own volition in any family proceedings if the court considers it appropriate (s.5(2)).

Appointments of guardians may be revoked or disclaimed. Revocation of a simple appointment may be by a further appointment under s.5(3) or (4); by a will or codicil; by destruction of the appointing instrument with the intention of revocation (s.6(3)); or by a written, signed and dated instrument (s.6(1)). Again, a person who signs on behalf of the revoker must do so in his presence and also that of two witnesses who each attest the signature (s.6(2)).

A guardian may disclaim his or her appointment by written instrument (s.6(5)).

The court has power to bring guardianship to an end on the application of a person who has parental responsibility for the child, the child concerned (with leave of the court) or of its own volition in any family proceedings.

Welfare reports. Under s.7 of the Act, the court may require a welfare report when considering any question with respect to a child under the Act. This effectively makes a report available in all proceedings brought under the Act. The content of a welfare report is to be more accessible in evidence. Under s.7(4) the court may take account of any statement in the report, and any evidence given in respect of matters referred to in the report, so far as they are relevant to the question being considered. Reports will be requested from an officer of the local authority, a probation officer, or any other person considered appropriate by the local authority.

Part II
Section 8 orders. Under ss.8 to 14 of the Act, there are four possible orders (called 'section 8 orders') which can be made in family proceedings where a question arises with respect to the welfare of any child, (impliedly therefore, not necessarily the child who is the subject of the proceedings). There is considerable power here because the court may make these orders on the application of anyone entitled, or who has leave to apply under s.10, or of its own volition, even though there has been no application. For example, it

is quite possible for a parent to bring proceedings for maintenance for a child, C; then, in these family proceedings, if the welfare of C is in issue, the other parent may ask for a contact order in respect of C, and if the question of the welfare of C's sister D arises, the court could also order contact with D at the same time. Practitioners should be aware that by bringing family proceedings in these circumstances, it is possible to open up the question of section 8 orders in relation to other children of that family where their welfare is in issue.

In order to better understand section 8 orders, one must first know the definition of 'family proceedings' in s.8(3) and (4). Basically, this term includes any proceedings under the inherent jurisdiction of the High Court, and under specified enactments including Parts I, II and IV of the Children Act 1989, the Matrimonial Causes Act 1973, the Domestic Violence and Matrimonial Proceedings Act 1976, the Domestic Proceedings and Magistrates' Courts Act 1978, and the Adoption Act 1976.

There are four new orders available under section 8:

(a) Contact order. This requires that the person with whom a child lives or is to live allows the child to visit or stay with the person named in the order or otherwise have contact. It replaces access, but is wider than the previous access orders, because contact could include letters, telephone calls, presents and other forms of communication.

(b) Prohibited steps order. An order that no step which would be taken by a parent in meeting his parental responsibility for a child, and which is of a kind specified in the order, shall be taken by any person without leave of the court.

(c) Specific issue order. An order giving directions for the purpose of determining a specific issue which has arisen, or may arise in connection with any aspect of parental responsibility for a child.

(d) Residence order. An order settling the arrangements to be made as to the person with whom a child is to live. This replaces previous orders for legal custody, joint custody, custody and/or care and control, and custodianship. Those who are entitled under s.10(5) to apply for a residence or contact order are: any party to a marriage in relation to whom the child is a child of the family (thus including step-parents); anyone with whom the child has lived for at least three years; anyone who has the consent of all those with a residence order in respect of the child; anyone who has the consent of the local authority if the child is in care; or anyone who has the consent of all those with parental responsibility for the child.

The principles upon which section 8 orders are to be made are set out in s.11, and because one of the intentions of the Act is to ameliorate the delays that can occur in child cases, the court may take responsibility for timing the progress of the case.

An interesting innovation is the power of the court to make a residence order in favour of more than one person, dividing the time a child lives with each, e.g., with one parent in term time, and the other in the holidays (s.11(4)).

There is a provision that the court shall not make a section 8 order which is intended to last beyond the child's 16th birthday, unless the circumstances of the case are exceptional.

There are restrictions on the making of section 8 orders. A residence order is the only one which can be made with respect to a child in care, and, if made, will discharge the care order. This opens the way for those entitled to apply for a residence order to make the application to the court, thus endeavouring to obtain a discharge of the care order, but there are safeguards in the Act – see below in the discussion of Part IV.

A local authority may not apply for residence or contact orders (s.9(2)).

Local-authority foster-parents are restricted in the circumstances in which they can apply for section 8 orders under s.9(3); and there are time-limits on subsequent applications, see the discussion of Part XII below.

Those who have a residence order in their favour may not remove the child from the jurisdiction of the court, nor change the child's surname without written consent of those with parental responsibility or leave of the court (s.13).

Family assistance orders. Under s.16, the court has the power to require a probation officer or local authority officer to 'advise, assist and (where appropriate) befriend' any named person, who could be the child, his or her parent or guardian, or any person with whom the child lives. The order can only be made in exceptional circumstances, and with the consent of those named in the order. It may last for up to six months.

Part III Local Authority Support for Children and Families
This part, together with sch. 2 to the Act, sets out the duty of local authorities in supporting children and families. The basic premise underlying the Act seems to be that children are usually better off with their own families if at all possible, and that parents should take on board the responsibility for their children, with assistance where it is needed.

There is a duty under s.17 to 'safeguard and promote the welfare' and to 'promote the upbringing' of 'children in need', defined in s.17(10) as those who are 'unlikely to achieve or maintain a reasonable standard of health or development . . . without the provision . . . of services' and those whose 'health or development is likely to be significantly impaired, or further impaired, without the provision . . . of services' and those who are disabled. The last category includes those who are blind, deaf, dumb, suffering from mental disorder, or substantially and permanently handicapped by illness, injury or congenital deformity.

As part of their general duty under s.17 to provide a range and level of services appropriate for children in need, local authorities are to provide day care as appropriate for children under five who are not yet attending school (s.18). Along with this goes training, advice and counselling for those caring for or accompanying children in day care.

Accommodation must be provided under s.20, where required for children in need, in circumstances specified in that section.

There is a general duty to identify children in need, and to keep a register of disabled children. Information about the services available must be published and steps taken to ensure that the information is received by those it may benefit. The emphasis is on prevention of problems by more careful monitoring of the locality, with a view to reducing, *inter alia*, care and supervision proceedings and criminal offences by or concerning children.

Where children are living away from home, in police detention or on remand in respect of criminal offences, the local authority must provide suitable accommodation (s.21).

For other children being looked after by a local authority, suitable accommodation, maintenance, advice and assistance, must be provided, having ascertained the wishes of the child, parents, and non-parents with parental responsibility for the child, or anyone else whose wishes are considered to be relevant (ss.22 to 24). For the first time, the Act recognises the need to be aware of the child's religious persuasion, racial origin, cultural and linguistic background.

Where a local authority is looking after a child, he or she may not be placed or kept in secure accommodation unless it is necessary, and then only in the situations outlined in s.25.

The remainder of Part III deals with review of cases, cooperation and consultation between authorities, and recoupment of costs of providing services. Parents, or the child herself, or a family member receiving services may be asked to pay for certain services provided by a local authority, unless they are on family credit or income support under the Social Security Act 1986.

Part IV Care and Supervision
Care orders. The Act, in s.31, creates a completely new ground for care. The court may only make an order where it is satisfied that (a) the child concerned is suffering, or is likely to suffer, significant harm; and (b) that the harm or likelihood of harm is attributable to either (i) the care given to the child, or likely to be given to him if the order were not made, not being what it would be reasonable to expect a parent to give to him; or (ii) the child's being beyond parental control.

On an application for care, the court may alternatively order supervision and vice versa. The grounds are the same for both, and must be satisfied before either order can be made.

The terms used, 'harm', 'development', 'health' and 'ill-treatment', are defined in s.31(9) for the avoidance of doubt, and s.31(10) states that where the question of whether harm suffered by a child is significant turns on the child's health or development, his health or development shall be compared with that which could reasonably be expected of a similar child.

The Act imposes a duty on the courts to have regard to the general principle that any delay in disposing of an application will prejudice the welfare of the child. The court shall draw up a timetable for the action and see that it is adhered to so far as is reasonably practicable. The effect of a care order is to impose on the local authority a duty to receive the child into its care, and to give that authority parental responsibility for the child. The child's surname may not be changed, nor may the child be removed from the United Kingdom (save for one month) without the consent of all who have parental responsibility for the child or leave of the court (s.33(7)).

There is a new provision in the Act: that parents, guardians and those with a residence order in their favour in respect of a child in care shall be allowed reasonable access. Access to a child in care will no longer be at the discretion of the local authority as it was formerly. Access may only be refused where it is not in the child's interests or the child's welfare to allow it. A local authority may only refuse access in the child's interests for a limited period of seven days. Otherwise, an order of the court is required authorising the authority to refuse access. Such an order may be made at the same time as a care order.

Supervision orders. Parts I and II of sch. 3, read together with s.35 of the Act make changes to the previous legislation and set out the nitty-gritty of the operation of supervision orders. The grounds for the making of a supervision order (placing the child under the supervision of a designated local authority or, in certain circumstances, a probation officer) have been mentioned above. In addition, the Act gives power to the court to include requirements in a supervision order for the child or a 'responsible person' (a person with parental responsibility for the child or with whom the child was living) to take a particular course of action. This is new. Previously, requirements could be made of the child only. Other possible requirements are intermediate treatment, psychiatric and medical examinations in specified circumstances, and psychiatric or medical treatment, again in specified circumstances.

The old law did not permit supervision by a probation officer of a child under 13 years, but this seems now possible.

Previously, supervision could be ordered for three years by the court, but now, the supervision will automatically cease after one year, unless extended. It will still not be extended beyond a three-year period, or the child's 18th birthday, whichever occurs earlier.

Education supervision orders. Education supervision orders are a further innovation. Care orders are no longer available specifically for truancy. Instead, the local education authority have the power in s.36(1) to apply for an education supervision order, on the grounds that the child is of compulsory school age and is not being properly educated (i.e., he or she is not receiving education suited to age, ability, aptitude and any special needs he or she may have). Note, though, that if the failure of the child to attend school is causing or likely to cause significant harm to the child, then a care order may still be sought.

An education supervision order may last for one year, after which it will automatically expire unless renewed. There is no limit on the number of renewals permitted, and an extension may be granted for a period of up to three years, but the order ceases on the child no longer being of compulsory school age (16 at present), or on the making of a care order. Details are set out in sch.3, part III.

The court may not make a care or supervision order of its own volition. If appropriate, it may ask the local authority to investigate the circumstances in which the child is living, and report to the court. The local authority may then, as a result of their investigation, apply for care or supervision (s.37).

Interim orders. Where care or supervision proceedings are adjourned, under s.38, the court may make an interim order, if satisfied that there are reasonable grounds for believing that the care or supervision grounds exist in relation to the child. There are time-limits on the duration of interim orders, and the court may make specific directions as to medical or psychiatric examination or other assessment on making the order. The directions may be negative, forbidding examinations or assessments considered unnecessary by the court (s.38(7)).

The first interim care order may not last longer than eight weeks. A subsequent interim order may not last for more than four weeks, unless the first interim order was made less than four weeks previously. If this is the case, then the second or subsequent interim order(s) may last until a date eight weeks from that of the first order (s.38).

Examples
Interim Order 1, eight weeks. Order 2, four weeks.
Interim Order 1, three weeks. Order 2, maximum five weeks.
Interim Order 1, one week. Order 2, three weeks. Order 3, four weeks.

STATUTES

Interim Order 1, four weeks. Order 2, four weeks.

Guardians ad litem. There are wide powers in ss.41 to 43 for the court to appoint a guardian *ad litem* and, unless the court considers it unnecessary to make an appointment in the child's interests, it seems that a guardian *ad litem* will be appointed in most cases involving care or supervision, both in cases under Part V of the Act (see below) and other specified proceedings. The guardian *ad litem* will have the right of access to local authority records, and any copies made shall be admitted as evidence of any matter referred to in the guardian *ad litem's* report or evidence given in those proceedings.

Part V Protection of Children
Child assessment orders. These are entirely new orders which can be made by the court under s.43 of the Act on the application of an authorised person, i.e., a local authority or NSPCC officer. Where the court is satisfied that the applicant has reasonable cause to suspect that the child is suffering or likely to suffer significant harm, it may order an assessment of the state of the child's health or development, or the way in which the child is being treated, in order to determine whether or not the child is suffering or is likely to suffer significant harm. The order can only be made where it is unlikely that the assessment would be successful, or made at all, without the order.

Emergency protection order. Sections 44 and 45 of the Act provide for the emergency protection of children. The court may make an emergency protection order if satisfied that there is reasonable cause to believe that a child will suffer significant harm if not removed to accommodation provided by or on behalf of the applicant for the order (usually the local authority), or if he does not remain in the place in which he is then being accommodated.

The making of the order immediately gives the applicant parental responsibility for the child, authorises his removal to or retention in, the appropriate accommodation, and operates as a direction to those in a position to do so to comply with the order (s.44).

The court may give directions with regard to medical or psychiatric examination of the child, and contact with named people. This has obvious advantages in child abuse cases, and clears up a previous problem of authorisation of medical examinations, giving control to the court (s.44(6)). The applicant must return the child to the previous carer, or to a parent, person with parental responsibility, or other appropriate person if he considers it safe to do so. Further leave of the court is not required to return the child (s.44(10) and (11)). During the existence of the emergency protection order, the child may again be removed if necessary (s.44(12)).

There is a requirement that the applicant shall allow contact (unless otherwise directed by the court), during the subsistence of an emergency protection order, between child and parents, those with parental responsibility, those with whom the child lived before the order, and others with contact orders in force in relation to the child (s.44(13)). This is a welcome addition to the legislation in that contact between child and parents or carers is recognised as important and is now the subject of a requirement rather than an issue left to the discretion, usually, of the local authority.

Another important change is the alteration in the duration of the emergency protection order, to a maximum of eight days (s.45). One extension only, for a period up to a maximum of seven days, may be granted by the court if it is satisfied, on reasonable grounds, that the applicant is not ready to apply for a care order, and that the child would be likely to suffer significant harm if the order were not extended.

There is power under the Act when making an emergency protection order, to order disclosure of the child's whereabouts (s.48(1)) and authorise entry and/or search of premises to find that child (s.48(3)) or another child (s.48(4)). The applicant may be accompanied by a nurse, doctor or health visitor (s.45(12)). Obstruction of such an order or authorisation is an offence punishable under s.48(7) and (8) by a fine of level 3 on the standard scale. Under s.48(9) to (11), where refusal of entry is anticipated or has occurred, the court may grant a warrant authorising the police to assist the person attempting to exercise powers under an emergency protection order. A nurse, health visitor or medical practitioner may be directed to accompany the constable executing the warrant.

Police protection. A police constable may remove a child from danger, or prevent his removal from a safe place in cases of emergency. This is referred to in the Act as 'police protection' (s.46).

STATUTES

The police cannot just whisk a child away into oblivion. There are safeguards in this section in that the police have to inform the local authority as soon as is reasonably practicable, and the child must be taken on to local authority accommodation if he or she had first been taken elsewhere by the police. The police constable must tell the child personally what is happening, if he or she is capable of understanding, and, as soon as reasonably practicable, tell the child's parents or anyone with parental responsibility for that child, or anyone with whom the child was living immediately before he or she was taken into police protection. The reasons for the police protection must be given, and the protection has a time-limit of 72 hours. The case must be reported to the chief officer of the police area concerned for investigation. Contact should be allowed by the constable between the child, and his or her parents, those with contact orders or parental responsibility for the child, and those with whom the child was living before the police protection took place. Anyone who intentionally obstructs any person exercising the power of entry and search under this section will be guilty of an offence punishable on summary conviction by a fine not exceeding level 3 on the standard scale.

Abduction of children in care. Under s.49, a person will be guilty of an offence if, knowingly and without authority or reasonable excuse, he or she takes a child away from the 'responsible person', i.e., the person who for the time being has the care of the child under a care order, emergency protection order, or under police protection, as the case may be. It is also an offence to induce or incite a child to run away from care in these situations, or to keep such a child away from the responsible person.

The court may make a 'recovery order' under s.50, where there is reason to believe that the child in care has been abducted, is being unlawfully retained, has run away, or is missing. The recovery order operates as a direction, to any person who can do so, to produce the child on request to an authorised person, or alternatively enables an authorised person to remove the child and return him or her into care. There are provisions for disclosure of a child's whereabouts, entry and search using reasonable force, and an offence of intentional obstruction of an authorised person in exercising power under the section to remove a child, again punishable on summary conviction with a fine up to level 3.

Children's refuge. This part also creates, in s.51, the concept of a refuge for children at risk. Certain premises or foster homes may be granted a certificate by the Secretary of State, exempting them from the provisions of various enactments creating offences relating to the abduction or unlawful retention of a child in care. They will be known as refuges for children at risk.

Part VI Community Homes

The Act directs that local authorities shall make arrangements for the provision of community homes for the care and accommodation of children looked after by them. This part deals with the responsibility for the establishment and control of community homes.

Such homes will be under the ultimate control of the Secretary of State, who will have a right to authorise persons to inspect such homes, their records, and the children living there.

Part VII Voluntary Homes and Voluntary Organisations

This part sets out the controls on the accommodation of children by voluntary organisations. Voluntary homes must be registered (s.60), and they have a duty to safeguard the welfare of children they accommodate, to make such use of facilities available for children cared for by their own parents as is reasonable, and to advise, assist and befriend the child when he or she leaves the home (s.61).

The wishes of the child, parents, those with parental responsibility and others whose wishes are relevant shall be considered in making decisions with respect to the child. Local authorities have a duty to ensure that voluntary organisations providing accommodation for children in their area are safeguarding and promoting the welfare of the children living there (s.62), and the Secretary of State may make regulations requiring visits to check on children so accommodated. If the local authority are not satisfied as to the welfare of any child in a voluntary home, they must take steps (unless it is not in the child's interests to do so) to return the child to parents, people with parental responsibility for him, relatives, or consider the exercise of their own functions with respect to the child (s.62).

Part VIII Registered Children's Homes

Sections 63 to 65 deal with the compulsory registration of children's homes. Registration is compulsory in the sense that no child may be accommodated in a children's home unless it is registered. A home is a children's home if it provides accommodation for more than three children at any one time. There are exceptions to these provisions, the most obvious of which is the home of the children's parents. Other exceptions include community or voluntary homes, hospitals, residential care and nursing homes, and certain independent schools.

The person carrying on a home accommodating children without registration in contravention of s.63 commits an offence punishable by a maximum fine of level 5. There is a duty to safeguard the welfare of the children living in such homes, and certain people will be disqualified from carrying on such homes under s.65. Contravention of the provisions of s.65 is an offence punishable by a maximum of six months' imprisonment and/or a fine of level 5 on summary conviction.

Part IX Private Fostering
The Foster Children Act 1980 will be repealed and replaced by this Part of the Act. Basically, the Act brings private fostering arrangements into line with those made for children looked after by a local authority. Where a foster home has more than three children, it will be classed as a children's home, and will therefore require registration, unless it comes within exemptions specified in the Act. The definition of private fostering also takes into account the possibility that a temporary arrangement may be made by a person with parental responsibility for someone else to discharge his or her responsibilities, for example, while away on business or holiday. The maximum length of a temporary period set by s.66 is 28 days, after which the arrangement becomes one of private fostering, and therefore subject to the regulations in the Act.

Local authorities have a duty to safeguard the welfare of privately fostered children (s.67). The Secretary of State has power to make regulations concerning private fostering arrangements, and the local authority have power to visit premises in which children are so fostered.

Certain people may be disqualified from fostering privately under s.68, and local authorities have the power under s.69 to prohibit certain people from fostering children privately if they personally, or the premises in which they wish to foster, are considered unsuitable; or where it would be prejudicial to the welfare of the child to allow him to be accommodated by that person in those premises. Those living in the same household as a disqualified person may not foster privately, unless the local authority has given written consent. Breach of these provisions is an offence, under s.70, which creates a number of separate offences punishable by varying fines and terms of imprisonment.

Part X Child Minding and Day Care for Young Children
The previous law on these matters was based on the Nurseries and Child-Minders Regulation Act 1948, which will be repealed. Because young children are particularly vulnerable, local authorities have a duty to keep a watchful eye on day care and child-minding services provided in their area. The 'old' law is now re-enacted with amendments and modifications. The Act defines a child-minder as one who 'looks after one or more children under the age of eight, for reward' for a period or total periods exceeding two hours in any one day (s.71(2)). Day care is defined in s.71(2), and is similar, the distinction being that child minding occurs on domestic premises, whilst day care occurs on non-domestic premises.

Identification of those who provide child-minding or day-care services is vital, and therefore the Act imposes a duty on each authority to keep a register of those providing these services (s.71(1)). The local authority have power to refuse to register as a child-minder any person whom they consider to be unfit to care for children under eight, or to refuse registration if the domestic premises to be used are not fit for this use because of their condition, the condition of equipment there or the situation, structure or size of the premises (s.71(7) and (11)).

Similarly, an application for registration in the register of persons who provide day care may be refused if any person on the premises to which the application relates is considered unfit to care for children, or the premises themselves are unfit for the reasons outlined above (s.71(9) to (11)).

Refusal to register can be justified where a person deemed unfit lives or works at domestic premises to be used for child minding (s.71(8)).

Appeal lies to the court against a refusal or cancellation of registration, matters concerning requirements, or refusal of consent to employ a disqualified person under sch.11, para.2. The local authority are bound to give 14 days' advance notice of a decision so that the person affected has a chance to appeal (s.77).

The Act sets out a list of those who are exempt from the requirement for registration, including the child's parents, foster-parents, relatives, or those with parental responsibility for him. Certain nannies working in their employers' homes are exempt, even if they look after a child for two employers, provided they are working in one employer's home. Amusingly, the Act departs here from its usual practice of using 'he' throughout, and refers to 'she', presumably on the assumption that nannies are female. Billies' rights campaigners note!

Bearing in mind the welfare and safety of the children to be looked after, the Act empowers a local authority to impose requirements when registering a child-minder under s.72, as to, for example, the maximum number of children to be looked after, security, records etc. The Act is concerned, too, with the safety of the premises and the equipment used. Accurate records are needed to ensure compliance with the provisions of the Act.

Section 73 provides for similar requirements to be made of people providing day care.

Registrations may be cancelled under s.74 in circumstances that would have justified a refusal of registration; where the care provided is inadequate; where contravention of s.72 or s.73 has occurred; or where the annual fee is unpaid.

There is provision for an *ex parte* emergency application to the court for an order to cancel or vary a registration where a child or children being looked after are suffering or likely to suffer significant harm (s.75).

Premises used for child minding or day care may be inspected by the local authority at any reasonable time, and must be visited at least once each year (s.76). During these inspections, the inspector may look at the premises, the children there, arrangements for the children's welfare, and the records kept.

Part XI Secretary of State's Supervisory Functions
The Secretary of State has wide powers under the Act. In addition to the power to make orders and regulations in relation to the provisions of the Act, there is a further responsibility to oversee the arrangements made for the care and welfare of children by local authorities and by others.

Section 80 provides for the inspection of children's homes and other premises in which children are cared for, including not only residential care, but day care, child minding and fostering.

There is a power to require information and inspect records relating to these places, and to enter premises at any reasonable time. Failure to comply with this provision is a summary offence punishable with a fine of level 3 (s.80(10)).

Inquiries may be held under s.81 by the Secretary of State into any matter connected with the functions of the social services committee of a local authority, the functions of an adoption agency or the functions of a voluntary organisation or home for children. Detention of a child under Children and Young Persons Act 1933, s.53, may also be the subject of an inquiry. The Secretary of State has the power to give financial support to approved child care training, provision of secure accommodation by local authorities, and voluntary organisations for maintenance of voluntary homes (s.82).

There is a wide power to assist in or conduct research into matters which include the functions of local authorities in relation to children and mental health under specified enactments, adoption, and accommodation of children in residential care or nursing homes. Information may be sought, too, from the clerks of magistrates' courts about court proceedings relating to children. An abstract of the information gained through this research is to be laid before Parliament each year. Failure by a local authority to comply with the duties imposed on them under the Act may cause the Secretary of State to make a default order, enforceable by mandamus (s.84).

Part XII Miscellaneous and General
This part of the Act ties up the loose ends of the legislation.

Local authorities to be notified of children accommodated by health and local education authorities. Section 85 requires the notification to a local authority of any child provided with accommodation by a health authority or local education authority, and the local authority are under a duty to take steps to determine whether the child's welfare is adequately safeguarded, and to consider whether to exercise their functions under the Act with respect to the child.

Local authorities to be notified of children accommodated in residential care, nursing or mental nursing homes. Section 86 makes similar provisions in relation to children accommodated in residential care homes, nursing homes and mental nursing homes. Failure to comply with the section is a summary offence punishable by a maximum fine at level 3.

Independent schools. Section 87 ensures that the proprietors or those responsible for conducting independent schools have a duty to promote the welfare of the children there. It authorises inspection by the local authority for the area, of the accommodation provided for the children, records, and computer records. If it is felt that the school is not safeguarding the children's welfare, then the Secretary of State must be notified.

Obstruction of a local authority in the exercise of their powers under this section is a summary offence punishable by a maximum fine of level 3.

Paternity tests. The court already has power under Family Law Reform Act 1969 s.20, to order blood tests to establish (so far as is possible) paternity of a child. Section 89 extends that power to enable the court to make an order directing who is to carry out the tests. The direction may nominate the person named in the application or, where the court does not consider it appropriate to specify that person, it may decline to make the direction. In other words, the court may grant or refuse a direction, but does not have the power to make a nomination of its own volition.

Criminal care and supervision orders. Under the former law, a child who committed an offence could be the subject of care or supervision proceedings under Children and Young Persons Act 1969, s.1(2)(f) (colloquially known as the 'offence condition'), or the child could be the subject of criminal proceedings. If found by the juvenile court in criminal proceedings to have committed the offence, or having admitted the offence, the child could be placed in care or under supervision by the juvenile court. Care could be ordered in criminal proceedings if the offence was one which in the case of an adult would be punishable by imprisonment. The idea behind this was that a child committing serious offences was very likely to be lacking in social and behavioural development and in need of some sort of care and control. The Act removes the power to make care orders in criminal proceedings, and also abolishes the 'offence condition'. Schedule 12, para.23, creates a replacement provision (adding a new s.12AA to the Children and Young Persons Act 1969): that in criminal proceedings, where the child is already subject to a supervision order imposed for an offence, a requirement may be included in a supervision order that the child reside in local authority accommodation for a period of up to six months. There are safeguards in that the offence must be one punishable by imprisonment in the case of an adult, and the circumstances in which the child was living must have contributed to commission of the offence.

This deprivation of liberty must not be imposed on a legally unrepresented child, unless he has had a chance to apply but has not done so, or has applied but been refused on financial grounds (s.12).

There are also provisions that cover the situation of a child in care under the 'old' legislation whilst the new provisions of the Act come into force. The period during which care will continue for children under 'criminal care' orders at the time that s.80 of the Act comes into force will be limited to six months from the date that section comes into effect.

Effect and duration of orders. Section 91 sets out the provisions regarding the duration of orders under the Act. See table 1.1.

Appeals. Section 94 governs appeals and orders which may be made on appeal. Appeal from the magistrates' court lies to the High Court. Formerly, in care cases, the Crown Court (with therefore judges experienced in mainly criminal law) heard appeals from the juvenile care court. Now, the move is towards a more satisfactory situation whereby cases involving children will be heard by justices and judges who have experience in child law and practice, with specialist training. It remains for rules to be made by the Lord Chancellor to provide for appeals relating to the transfer of cases within 'the court'.

Attendance of child before the court. Section 95 empowers the court in proceedings under Part IV (care and supervision) or Part V (protection of children) to order the child to attend any part of those

STATUTES

Table 1.1 Effect and duration of orders under Children Act 1989

Order	Discharged by					
Wardship	Age 18	Care order				
Care	Age 18		Residence order	Supervision order		Adoption
Supervision	Age 18	Care order		Further supervision order		Adoption
Guardianship	Age 18					Adoption
Parental responsibility	Age 18					Adoption
Residence	Age 16	Care order	Further residence order			Adoption	Parents living together for six months
Contact	Age 16	Care order				Adoption	Parents living together for six months
Specific issue	Age 16	Care order				Adoption	
Prohibited steps	Age 16	Care order				Adoption	
School attendance		Care order					

proceedings. The order may authorise a constable to bring the child to court, and to enter premises and search for the child if necessary. The court may also order disclosure of information about the child's whereabouts by anyone believed to have that knowledge.

Evidence relating to or given by children. Section 96 enables a child's evidence to be heard by the court, even if he or she does not understand the nature of an oath, provided that the duty to tell the truth is understood, and the child has sufficient understanding to justify the evidence being heard (s.96(1) and (2)).

In civil cases involving children, in the past the hearsay rule was often not strictly applied. However, as a result of two recent cases, *Re H (A Minor) and K* v *K, The Times,* 9 June 1989, in which the Court of Appeal held that in the matrimonial jurisdiction the hearsay rule must be applied, this leeway now may be curtailed. The juvenile court is presently governed by the Evidence Act 1938, and there is a risk that a stricter interpretation may now be applied in care cases. The Act empowers the Lord Chancellor to make orders providing for the admissibility of hearsay evidence in civil proceedings in relation to evidence in connection with the upbringing, maintenance or welfare of a child (s.96(3)). Statements rendered admissible may be in prescribed form or recorded by a prescribed method, including video or sound tape recording.

The privacy of children is respected in the Act (s.97, restricting publications and broadcasting).

There has been to date a rule which protected those who felt that certain evidence would incriminate them, enabling them to refuse to answer questions or give certain evidence. Section 98 removes that privilege in any proceedings under Part IV (care and supervision) or Part V (protection of children). In future, questions, incriminating or not, must be answered, and evidence given. However, there is an indemnity in the section in order to encourage frankness in the interests of the child. The section provides that a statement or admission in such proceedings shall not be admissible in any criminal proceedings for any offence other than perjury, against the person making it or that person's spouse (s.98(2)).

Legal aid. Legal aid will be available for proceedings under the Act. Being civil legal aid, it will be administered by the Legal Aid Board. In child cases, legal aid should be administered with as little delay as possible.

Section 99 amends the Legal Aid Act 1988 (see chapter 2), empowering the Lord Chancellor to make such further orders as he considers necessary or expedient, and waiving the provisions of ss.27, 28 and 30(1) and (2) of that Act. The effect of this seems to be that there will be no consideration of the merits of the case in advance of granting legal aid to parties to the proceedings or to the child. Legal aid may also be granted on an emergency basis in care and supervision proceedings before the statement of means has been considered.

Local authorities (and other prescribed bodies) may not have legal aid for representation in proceedings under the Act (s.99(2)).

Proceedings for variation or discharge of supervision orders (still available in criminal proceedings under the Children and Young Persons Act 1969), or appeals in respect of such orders, will now, under s.99(3), be included in Legal Aid Act 1988, s.19(5).

Where a child seeks legal representation in respect of proceedings brought under s.25 of the Act (secure accommodation for restricting liberty), it must be granted (s.99(2)).

Wardship. The High Court wardship jurisdiction has been severely curtailed by s.100 of the Act. Family Law Reform Act 1969, s.7 (enabling the High Court to place a child in the care or supervision of a local authority), ceases to have effect. The High Court cannot use its inherent jurisdiction to place a child in care, or under the supervision of a local authority; nor to require a child to be placed in local authority accommodation; nor can it give power to a local authority to determine any issue arising in connection with parental responsibility for a child. Section 100 forbids the High Court to use its inherent jurisdiction to make a child who is the subject of a care order a ward of court.

Effectively, a local authority seeking a care order will have to go through the care proceedings laid down in Part IV of the Act, and before making a care order the court must first be satisfied of the grounds laid down in the Act. The wardship jurisdiction is no longer any use as an avenue of appeal against an unsatisfactory magistrates' court decision in care proceedings, nor an avenue for resolution of any difficulties over access to a child in care. If, in wardship, the High Court hears evidence which leads it to consider that care may be appropriate, then it must require the local authority to investigate the child's circumstances and report to the court. A care order may then be made on the application of the local authority to 'the court' only under the provisions of the Act.

Search warrants. Under s.102, search warrants may be granted by the court to authorise a constable to assist a person to exercise powers under the Act, using reasonable force where necessary. The constable may be accompanied by a nurse, health visitor or medical practitioner if he chooses.

The Schedules
There is insufficient space to set out here the contents of the 15 schedules in any detail. Many of them relate to parts of the Act already discussed above, and have been mentioned in the text. Others relate to transitional provisions and consequential amendments. Much of the content of the schedules re-enacts former provisions with minor amendments. Some of the more major changes are discussed below.

Schedule 1 Financial Provisions
Financial relief for children is still available in divorce or nullity proceedings under the Matrimonial Causes Act 1973; and in the magistrates' court under the Domestic Proceedings and Magistrates' Courts Act 1978.

Further parts of the Family Law Reform Act 1987 have recently been brought into force, and these are discussed below at page 45.

Section 15 of and sch. 1 to the Act primarily re-enact, with modifications, the provisions of the Guardianship of Minors Act 1971, the Guardianship Act 1973, the Children Act 1975 and ss.15 and 16 of the Family Law Reform Act 1987, making financial relief available for children. The Act uses the old legislation to establish an improved basis for financial provision, clarifies some of the issues, and extends the power of the court. These provisions give power for the court to make financial provision for children on the application of a parent, guardian or person with a residence order in force in his or her favour with respect to the child. 'Parent' includes step-parents, and, similarly, orders may be made against step-parents, with safeguards. The court in making such an order against a step-parent will have to take into account the responsibility assumed by that step-parent for the child.

An application may be made for financial relief by anyone with a residence order in force in his or her favour with respect to the child, so this may include non-relatives and other carers (sch.1, para.1(1)).

The court does not have to wait for an application; it may make an order of its own volition when making, varying or discharging a residence order (sch.1, para.1(6)). The Act also enables the court to vary or revoke orders for financial relief made under other enactments (sch.1, para.8).

Adult children (those over 18) may apply for financial relief against a parent or step-parent for periodical payments or a lump-sum payment, in specified circumstances, e.g., when undergoing training or education or where special circumstances justify the application (sch.1, para.2). There can be no application, however, where the parents of the applicant are living together.

The Act makes available a wide range of orders, to deal with periodical payments (secured or unsecured, lump sums, and transfer or settlement of property. The jurisdiction of the courts is set out in the schedule, as are guidelines for the exercise of the court's discretion in making orders (sch.1, para.4(1)).

The Act empowers local authorities to spend money for the benefit of a child in many ways: contributions towards the cost of maintaining a child if living with a person who is not a parent or step-parent under a residence order (sch.1, para.15), money to promote the welfare of children in need and their families (sch.2, para.8), provision of family centres (sch.2, para.9) and promotion of contact between a child being looked after by the local authority and his or her family, including payment of travelling expenses to visit such a child. The Act also enables the local authority to claim contributions from liable relatives of a child, or from the child himself, if the child is over 16 years old.

Schedules 10 and 15 Adoption
Parts of the existing adoption law are unclear and the Act has gone a little way to clarify it and create a more cohesive structure. Schedule 10 contains a number of amendments to the Adoption Act 1976, which bring the 1976 Act into line with current legislation, but there are no really major changes because there is at present an intention to review and revise adoption law. Some of the provisions of the Adoption Act 1976 are repealed by sch.15.

If adoption proceedings are brought, now, under the Act, they will be classed under s.8(4)(d) as family proceedings, and therefore under the provisions of s.8, any order under that section may be made at any time during the adoption proceedings. If, during the proceedings (for example, on hearing the evidence), the court considers that care or supervision may be appropriate, then it may ask the local authority (under s.37(1)) to investigate the child's circumstances and report to the court. The local authority must consider whether any action should be taken with respect to the child (s.37(2)). and this would include care or supervision, or the provision of assistance to the child or to the child's family. The court may not make a care or supervision order under s.31 of its own volition, but if the local authority make the appropriate application, the court may then consider what order, if any, it should make. The former power of the court to order care in exceptional circumstances in proceedings such as these is no longer available.

There has been a movement towards the concept that if a child is looked after by a local authority or a voluntary organisation it is to assist the parent(s) of the child, and not as a step towards taking the child away from his or her family. Parents are to be encouraged to take responsibility for their children, and the idea of placing a child with a local authority would, hopefully, carry less fear and stigma about it; rather being seen as a step towards helping parents and keeping the family together if possible. In view of this, it is to be easier to obtain the return of a child who is being looked after by a local authority, and the former threat of a 'parental rights resolution' has gone.

The restrictions made by the Act on the powers of local authorities affect many areas of child law, including adoption. An application to free a child for adoption may only be made by an adoption agency (which would include a local authority or a voluntary organisation) in respect of a child in their care with the consent of the child's parents; or, if the child is in the care of the agency, being a local authority, under a care order. This means that children being looked after by a voluntary organisation or a local authority, but not under a care order, may not become the subject of an application for a freeing order for adoption unless their parents consent.

There are provisions in sch.10 para.21, (which inserts a new s. 51A into the Adoption Act 1976) to enable the Registrar General to set up an Adoption Contact Register in two parts: Part 1 of adopted persons and Part 2 of the birth parents or relatives of those adopted. On payment of a small fee, entries may be made as appropriate in the register, enabling adopted people to obtain information with which to contact their families if they so wish. In order to have an entry on the Register, certain conditions specified in the schedule must be fulfilled. This is a safeguard against abuse of the facility.

Adoption Act 1976, s.51, is amended by substituting new subsections (3) to (7). The Registrar General must inform an applicant for information under s.51 that counselling services are available, and where. Counselling facilities similar to those already available in England and Wales will now be available outside England and Wales to obviate the former necessity of travelling to obtain counselling (sch.10, para.20).

Allowances will be payable under sch.10 para.25, to those who have adopted, or intend to adopt, children in pursuance of arrangements made by adoption agencies. The agencies may now make the payments without needing to first obtain the approval of the Secretary of State. The payments may be made under general regulations.

2

STATUTORY INSTRUMENTS

Legal Aid in Criminal and Care Proceedings (Costs) Regulations 1989

(SI 1989 No. 343)

Came into force April 1989
These regulations cover miscellaneous matters relating to the determination of solicitors' disbursements, claims for costs by solicitors in criminal and care proceedings, counsel's fees, and taxation matters including appeals to the taxing master and to the High Court.

After a few general provisions, there follows, quietly, a quite sweeping and potentially devastating provision relating to the timing of costs claims. Regulation 5 provides that 'no claim for costs in respect of work done under a legal aid order shall be entertained unless the solicitor submits it within three months of the conclusion of the proceedings to which the order relates'. Regulation 17 permits the extension of the time-limit by the appropriate authority, possibly in some cases accompanied by a reduction in costs. Such reductions would not, however, be made without affording the claiming solicitor or counsel a chance to be heard on the matter.

The work for which the claims may be made is set out in the regulations, together with three grades of fee-earner: (a) senior solicitor; (b) solicitor, legal executive or fee-earner of equivalent experience; (c) articled clerk or fee-earner of equivalent experience.

The thorny problem of disbursements is still dealt with on the basis of those disbursements 'reasonably incurred' being allowable; but specific provisions are there for distance of the court or the assisted person's residence from the solicitor, and the cost of transcripts for use in the Court of Appeal obtained otherwise than

STATUTORY INSTRUMENTS

through the Registrar – in both cases, the disbursements may be limited to those considered reasonable.

Counsel (even though not assigned under the legal aid order) may be instructed in the magistrates' court, but the total sum of the fees claimable may be limited to the sum payable to a solicitor had the case been conducted by a solicitor only. Counsel, too have a three-month limit on the claiming of fees, and the basis for calculating their fees at a standard rate is set out in sch. 2.

For work done after 1 April 1989 new rates of remuneration apply as set out in the regulations. The rates for criminal work are lower than those for child care work, implementing an earlier policy that child care should be sufficiently remunerated to attract (or retain) experienced practitioners in this field of work. The rates of remuneration for solicitors are set out in sch. 1.

Criminal cases: magistrates' court

Preparation	£36.50 per hour
Advocacy	£46.00 per hour
Attendance where counsel assigned	£24.50 per hour
Travelling and waiting	£20.50 per hour
Routine letters written and telephone calls	£2.85 per item (£2.95 for fee-earner whose office is in legal aid area 1, 13 or 14)

Care cases

Preparation	£44.00 per hour (£47.00 per hour for fee-earners whose offices are in legal aid areas 1, 13, or 14)
Advocacy	£53.00 per hour
Attendance at court where counsel assigned	£28.00 per hour
Travelling and waiting	£24.50 per hour
Routine letters written and telephone calls	

Crown Court criminal and Court of Appeal proceedings
Figures in brackets are for fee-earners whose offices are in legal aid areas 1, 13 or 14.

Preparation	Senior solicitor	£42.50 per hour (£45)
	Solicitor, legal executive etc.	£36.50 per hour (£38.75)
	Articled clerk etc.	£24.00 per hour (£28)
Advocacy	Senior solicitor	£53.00 per hour
	Solicitor	£46.00 per hour
Attendance at court where counsel assigned	Senior solicitor	£35.00 per hour
	Solicitor, legal executive, etc.	£27.50 per hour
	Articled clerk etc.	£17.00 per hour
Travelling and waiting	Senior solicitor	£20.50 per hour
	Solicitor, legal executive etc.	£20.50 per hour
	Articled clerk etc.	£10.25 per hour
Routine letters and telephone calls		£2.85 per item (£2.95)

Standard fees

Part II of sch. 1 creates standard fees. This is a relatively new departure for the criminal practitioner, and it will be interesting to see how this is applied in practice. The proceedings to which it applies are listed in para. 1(2) of the schedule:

(a) Committals for trial for offences on indictment of class 3 or 4 (in accordance with directions given under Supreme Court Act 1981, s.75).

(b) Commitals for trial where the trial was anticipated to last two days or less and in fact did last two days or less, including cases where no jury was sworn.

(c) Appeals against conviction.

(d) Appeals against sentence.

(e) Committals for sentence, including specified proceedings.

There is a proviso that the trial judge may, if dissatisfied with the solicitor's conduct of a case, or where he considers it appropriate to determine fees under reg. 6, order that the fees shall be so determined.

The classes of work in respect of which standard fees are payable are:

(a) Preparation, including routine letters and telephone calls.

(b) Advocacy in bail applications.
(c) Attendance at court (including waiting) where counsel assigned).
(d) Travelling except:

   (i) to undertake work where standard fee not payable,
   (ii) to undertake advocacy on bail applications.

Travelling includes waiting time in connection with preparation work.

Standard fees for preparation
London rates apply to those whose offices are in legal aid areas 1, 13 or 14.

Proceedings	Lower standard fee £	Lower fee limit £	Principal standard fee £	Upper fee limit £
Jury trial (including case prepared for trial where no jury sworn)	106	146	204	255
London rate	112.50	152	213	267
Guilty pleas	67	89	143	184
London rate	71	93	149	193
Apeals against conviction	41.50	56	125	190
London rate	43.50	58	130	199
Appeals against sentence	30.25	43	76	107
London rate	32	45	80	111
Committals for sentence	34.50	42	80	115
London rate	36.50	44	84	119
Advocacy for bail applications	21.50			
London rate	23			

Attendance at court where counsel assigned £17.75 per hour
Travelling £15 per hour

Appeals to the Crown Court in care matters are not included.

There are provisions for appeal by a solicitor claiming costs who is dissatisfied either with the scale applied to the specific case, or the 'reasonableness' of any specific amount allowed.

The standard fee for preparation and advocacy plus an extra allowance of 20% for each additional defendant is payable where the practitioner acts for more than one defendant in the same case. There is no addition to the standard fee for attendance at court and travelling.

There are now standard fees for listening to tape recordings of interviews under the Police and Criminal Evidence Act 1984:

One tape (at least 10 minutes' duration)	£20
Where more than one tape	£35 for each save the last, and the last tape, £20, if it lasts for 10 minutes or more

Counsel's fees

Counsel are also subject to the standard fee system. Standard fees are set out in a table in sch. 2, Part I.

The basic fee covers preparation and the first day's hearing, including conferences.

Refresher fees cover any day that the hearing continues, and includes conferences, applications and appearances.

Wtitten work fees cover advice on evidence, plea, appeal, case stated and other written work.

Appearance fees cover attendance at applications, appearances including bail applications and short conferences not covered by the basic or refresher fees. Attendance at a pre-trial review is not included.

The refresher fees are based on a full day (where a hearing begins before and ends after the luncheon adjournment, but before 5.30 p.m.; or begins after lunch but ends after 5.30 p.m.); or a half day (which is where the hearing begins and ends before lunch; or begins after lunch but ends before 5.30 p.m.).

Where the hearing begins before lunch and ends after 5.50 p.m. then a 'more than full day' fee is payable.

There are special arrangements for partly heard cases, and a payment of 20% in addition to the standard fee for additional defendants represented by the same counsel, on the same basis as for solicitors.

Standard fees for counsel

Proceedings	Basic fee (£)
Jury trials	180
Guilty pleas	95
Appeals against conviction	95
Appeals against sentence	60
Committals for sentence	60
Standard appearance fee	37
Standard refresher fees:	
Half day	66
Full day	127
More than full day	193
Standard written work fee	24

There is, further, a table of maximum fees for junior counsel and Queen's counsel, in sch. 2, Part II, see tables 2.1 and 2.2.

See also the notes (below) on the Legal Aid Act 1988 which came into force 1 April 1989. The above notes should be read in conjunction with those below on the Legal Aid in Criminal and Care Proceedings (General) Regulations 1989.

Legal Aid in Criminal and Care Proceedings (General) Regulations 1989

(SI 1989 No. 344)

Came into force April 1989
Parts I to VI deal with the general power to grant legal aid, and matters relating to the nitty-gritty of applications, procedure and review. The way in which contributions are to be assessed is set out clearly in Part III. Part V deals with the circumstances in respect of which the nature of representation allowable is decided.

Part VII deals specifically with care proceedings, and includes a guardian *ad litem* in the list of those entitled to apply for legal aid (although of course a guardian *ad litem* will not be expected to contribute to legal aid costs). The provisions of Parts I to VI apply to care proceedings in the same way as to other matters.

The basic regulations for the granting of legal aid have not radically changed. Legal aid may be granted on application to a justices' clerk in form 1, or orally to the court, but in each case

Table 2.1 Junior counsel

Court	Type of proceedings	Basic fee	Full day refresher fee	Subsidiary fees		
				Attendance at consultations, conferences & views	Written work	Attendance at pre-trial reviews, applications and other appearances
Magistrates' Court	All cases	Maximum amount: £419	Maximum amount: £145	£24 per hour Minimum amount: £12	Maximum amount: £46	Maximum amount: £84
Crown Court	Jury trials	Maximum amount: £488				
	Cases prepared for trial in which no jury is sworn	Maximum amount: £284				
	Guilty pleas	Maximum amount: £172	Maximum amount: £160	£28 per hour Minimum amount: £14	Maximum amount: £52	Maximum amount: £89
	Appeals against conviction	Maximum amount: £188				
	Appeals against sentence	Maximum amount: £96				
	Committals for sentence	Maximum amount: £96				

Table 2.2 Queen's counsel

Court	Type of proceedings	Basic fee	Full day refresher fee	Subsidiary fees		
				Attendance at consultations, conferences & views	Written work	Attendance at pre-trial reviews, applications and other appearances
Magistrates' Court	All cases	Maximum amount: £4,035	Maximum amount: £270	£47 per hour Minimum amount: £24	Maximum amount: £95	Maximum amount: £186
Crown Court	All cases	Maximum amount: £4,900	Maximum amount: £300	£53 per hour Minimum amount: £27	Maximum amount: £108	Maximum amount: £234

where a statement of means is required, this must be considered by the justices' clerk first.

An applicant must be notified of refusal of legal aid by the magistrates' court. Refusal is on the ground that it does not appear to the court or to the justices' clerk to be in the interests of justice to make the order, and/or that the disposable income and capital of the applicant render that person ineligible for legal aid. In the event of refusal, the regulations provide that the court or the justices' clerk shall determine the contribution which would have been payable, and that the application may be renewed, or, alternatively, there may be a request for review to the area committee.

There are provisions for obtaining legal aid for the Crown Court, and for the Court of Appeal and the House of Lords.

The authorisation of the area committee may be sought for expenditure in obtaining expert written reports or opinions, or indeed other written reports or opinions; and transcripts of shorthand notes or tape recordings of proceedings or police interviews. The authorisation of the area committee may be sought in cases where the legal aid order already provides for solicitor and counsel and practitioners wish to instruct a Queen's counsel alone (without a junior) or where any expenditure which is unusual in size or nature is contemplated. The area committee, on granting authorisation for the expenditure requested, may also state a maximum fee to be paid. If such expenditure is refused, the solicitor may not receive or be a party to the making of any payment for work done in connection with the proceedings save for payments from the legal aid fund, or expenses or fees incurred in preparing, obtaining or considering a report, opinion or further evidence, whether provided by an expert witness or otherwise, or bespeaking transcripts of notes of proceedings or tape recordings of police interviews.

There are specific provisions in Part VII relating to care proceedings, in addition to the provision including the guardian *ad litem* in the category of applicants. Regulation 24 (requiring a statement of means) does not apply where representation is granted under Part VII. A person who is a party to care proceedings because he or she has a contrary interest in those proceedings will not become liable to a contribution to the cost of representing the child in addition to the costs of his or her representation.

Part VII provides that emergency applications for legal aid under Child Care Act 1980, s. 12E, may be made orally to a justice of the peace entitled to sit in the juvenile court, who must, before granting legal aid, consider the applicant's statement of means. A statement of means may, in these circumstances, be provided orally or in writing.

Note, however, that in a new and excellent book entitled *An Introduction to the Children Act 1989*, published by HMSO (see chapter 5), there is comment that, in order for the Legal Aid Board to act swiftly, the merits test will be waived for those who are automatically parties to applications for care and supervision orders (including the child) and legal aid will be granted in advance of the means test on an emergency basis. Children Act 1989, s.99, amends parts of the Legal Aid Act 1988 (see chapter 1) and s.99 also repeals ss.27, 28 and 30(1) and (2) of the Legal Aid Act 1988, dealing with legal aid in care and other proceedings relating to children. These changes will only come into force, however, when the relevant provisions of the Children Act 1989 are implemented and the Child Care Act 1980 will then also be repealed.

Subject to the emergency provisions outlined above, legal aid applications in respect of care proceedings are much the same as in criminal matters, save for the fact that the regulations relating to applications for review and determination of reviews expressly do not apply to care matters. This seems to imply that if legal aid is refused in care proceedings then the matter ends there, and there is no right to go to the legal aid committee for review. One hopes that the courts will grant legal aid widely in care matters, and that this will not prove to be an onerous provision.

Applications for legal aid for appeals to the Crown Court follow the same procedure as applications for Crown Court proceedings: they are made orally to the Crown Court or to the juvenile court at the conclusion of the juvenile court proceedings, or to the appropriate officer of the Crown Court, or to the justices' clerk of the juvenile court.

See also the notes above on the Legal Aid Act 1988 which came into force on 1 April 1989. This should be read in conjunction with the notes on the Legal Aid in Criminal and Care Proceedings (Costs) Regulations 1989, above.

Blood Tests (Evidence of Paternity) (Amendment) Regulations 1989

(SI 1989 No. 776)

Came into force 1 June 1989
These regulations make amendments to the Blood Tests (Evidence of Paternity) (Amendment) Regulations 1971 and revoke the Blood Tests (Evidence of Paternity) (Amendment) Regulations 1985 and 1988.

The effect of these regulations is to increase the charges which may be made by blood samplers and blood testers under the 1971 regulations in respect of blood tests carried out for the purpose of determining paternity in civil proceedings. Regulation 3 alters the 1971 regulations in that it leaves the basis for charges by samplers unchanged, but replaces the basis of charging for testers. There is a new maximum charge for each sample tested, including the making of a report, thus permitting different charges (up to the maximum) for different tests. The range of blood tests currently available is no longer limited to simple blood group investigation. Some tests available, like DNA analysis, are quite expensive comparatively speaking and the new regulations by implication recognise this.

The charges are listed in Sch 2, which is summarised below.

Part I Samplers
Making arrangements for taking samples	£13.60
Further arrangements to give effect to a variation by the court of a direction	£13.60
Taking sample:	
from first subject	£13.60
from each subject after first	£6.80

Taking second or subsequent samples from one or more subjects:
one	£13.60
two	£20.40
three or more	£34.10

Part II Testers
Maximum charge to be made by a tester in respect of tests for the

purpose of giving effect to one direction shall be £115.90 (exclusive of VAT) for each sample tested, and no additional charge for the making of a report.

Child Abduction and Custody (Parties to Conventions) (Amendment) (No. 2) Order 1989

(SI 1989 No. 980)

Order made 13 June 1989
This order amends the Child Abduction and Custody (Parties to Conventions) Order 1986. It adds Norway and Sweden to the list of contracting States to the European Convention on Recognition and Enforcement of Decisions Concerning Custody of Children and on the Restoration of Custody of Children, signed at Luxembourg on 20 May 1980 (Cm 191).

Child Abduction and Custody (Parties to Conventions) (Amendment) (No. 3) Order 1989

(SI 1989 No. 1332)

Order made 2 August 1989
This order amends the Child Abduction and Custody (Parties to Conventions) Order 1986. It adds Belize to the list of contacting States to the Convention on the Civil Aspects of International Child Abduction signed at the Hague on 25 October 1980 (Cm 33).

Matrimonial Causes (Costs) (Amendment) Rules 1989

(SI 1989 No. 385)

Came into force 1 April 1989
Created under the Matrimonial Causes Act 1973 and the Family Law Act 1986, these rules substitute new provision for r. 11(1) and (3), together with sch. 2 of the Matrimonial Causes (Costs) Rules 1988.

The old r. 11(1) if replaced by the following provision:

(1) Subject to the following provisions of this rule, on any

STATUTORY INSTRUMENTS

taxation of the costs of a litigant in person there may be allowed such costs as would have been allowed if the work and disbursements to which the costs relate had been done or made by a solicitor on the litigant's behalf together with any payments reasonably made by him for legal advice relating to the conduct of or the issues raised by the proceedings.

The amendment to r. 11(3) is simply to raise the former sum of £6.50 to £7.00.

The replacement of sch. 2, however, creates more extensive changes. The sums allowed on preparation, conferences with counsel, attendances, and junior counsels' fees, are amended and the new amounts are reproduced below.

Taxation allowances altered by Part V of the new Schedule, are also reproduced below.

Part I   Preparation

Item	High Court	County Court
Writing routine letters	£3.50	£3.00
Receiving routine letters	£1.75	£1.50
Routine telephone calls	£3.50	£3.00
Other preparation work including interviews, gathering evidence, perusal and consideration of documents, and non-routine telephone calls	**Divorce Registry or South-Eastern Circuit** £38.50 per hour	£32 per hour
	All other circuits £36 per hour	£32 per hour
General care and conduct allowance	50%	50%
Travelling and waiting	£26.50 per hour	£24.50 per hour

Part II   Conferences with Counsel

Attending counsel in conference	£31 per hour	£27 per hour
Travelling and waiting	£26.50 per hour	£24.50 per hour

Part III   Attendances

With counsel at trial, hearing, appointment or application	£31 per hour	£27 per hour
Without counsel at trial, hearing, appointment or application	£46 per hour	£43 per hour
Travelling and waiting	£26.50 per hour	£24.50 per hour

Part IV Fees for Junior Counsel

Item	High Court	County Court
Unopposed application for injunction standard fee or on procedural issue	£74	£65
	maximum fee	
	£122	£106
Brief on trial, or ancillary application, or children appointment depending on length:		
One hour	standard fee	
	£110	£95
	maximum fee	
	£223	£191
Half day	standard fee	
	£154	£133
	maximum fee	
	£254	£233
Full day	standard fee	
	£307	£265
	maximum fee	
	£488	£424
More than one full day	discretionary	
Each day (or part of day) after first day	discretionary	
Conference standard fee		
	£17 per ½ hour	£15 per ½ hour
Complex written work (advice on evidence, opinions, requests for answers, affidavits)	£80 per item	£69 per item
Other written work	£48 per item	£42 per item
Travelling time	£15.40 per hour	£13.20 per hour plus expenses

Note that these fees for travelling do not apply where the court is within 25 miles of Charing Cross or where there is no local Bar in the court town, or within 25 miles thereof.

Part V Taxation

Preparing the bill, and completing taxation	£26.50–£74	£26.50–£42.50

Note that preparing for and attending the taxation is not included here.

Preparing for and attending taxation	discretionary
Review by registrar or judge (including preparation)	discretionary

STATUTORY INSTRUMENTS

Matrimonial Causes (Costs) (Amendment No. 2) Rules 1989

(SI 1989 No. 1021)

Came into force 10 July 1989
These rules amend the Matrimonial Causes (Costs) (Amendment) Rules 1989 so as to make it clear that those rules apply only to the taxation of costs of work done on or after 1 April 1989.

Children and Young Persons (Amendment) Act 1986 (Commencement No. 2) Order 1988

(SI 1989 No. 2188)

Came into force 1 June 1989
This order adds a new s. 22A(1) to the Child Care Act 1980 empowering the Secretary of State to make regulations governing the accommodation of children in care when they are in the charge of a parent, or guardian, a relative, or other person, e.g. a friend. When the Children Act 1989 comes into force the Child Care Act 1980 will be replaced by new provisions. Please see chapter 1 for further discussion of the provisions of the Children Act 1989.

Accommodation of Children (Charge and Control) Regulations 1988

(SI 1988 No. 2183)

Came into force 1 June 1989
These regulations require that local authorities take on board the responsibility for consultation with relevant agencies, and inspection of the premises in which a child is to live before a child in care is placed to reside with parents or others. There is considerable tightening up of the arrangements for the supervision by the local authority of such a child's health and welfare, and there are requirements to check regularly the child's progress and to keep case records and also registers of these placements outside local authority accommodation. When the Children Act 1989 comes into force, these provisions will be replaced by those of the Act.

See chapter 1 for further information.

Boarding Out of Children (Foster Placement) Regulations 1988

(SI 1988 No. 2184)

Came into force 1 June 1989
These regulations replace the earlier Boarding Out of Children Regulations 1955 (SI 1955, No. 1377) and the Boarding Out of Children (Amendment) Regulations 1982 (SI 1982 No. 447).

It is increasingly becoming recognised that children placed with carers outside their family need support, as do the carers themselves. Foster-parents have to work at establishing and maintaining a relationship with the children they care for, with social services, and also very frequently with the parents and family of the fostered child. This is no easy task. These regulations are made with the needs of the children and families concerned, the authorities and the foster-parents in mind.

They apply to the boarding out of children by local authorities and voluntary organisations, excluding children placed for adoption: regs 1 and 2.

Under reg 3. and sch. 1, the local authority or the voluntary organisation is required to approve the household into which the child will be placed, to review the situation at regular intervals, and, before giving approval, to obtain particulars of proposed foster-parents and to interview referees named by them.

Regulation 4 requires the authorities to see that the child has a medical examination and assessment before his or her placement there and to ensure that there are regular medical examinations of the children in foster placements.

Regulation 5 sets out to establish a coherent statement of the duties of the authorities in respect of foster placements, and reg. 6 and sch. 2 make provision for written contracts between authorities and the foster-parents. In this way, both the authorities and the foster-parents know what to expect of each other. The duties and undertakings of the foster-parents are clearly defined, and they know what they can expect to receive by way of support.

Under reg. 7, notice of a placement must be given by the authority to the child's parent, guardian or custodian. Provision must be

STATUTORY INSTRUMENTS 43

made for visits by the authority to the fostered child, and also for access to the fostered child by his or her family. This is a matter for discretion to be decided within the Code of Practice on Access to Children in Care (made under the Child Care Act 1980, s. 12 G(a)). Note that when the Children Act 1989 is implemented, the Child Care Act 1980 will be repealed and the provisions of the Children Act 1989 will replace it, see chapter 1.

Regulation 8 requires the local authority to supervise placements, and requires regular visits to the child. There are, too, matters to be taken into account in making a placement, including the views of the child himself, the parent or guardian, and those of the foster-parents.

Regulation 9 deals with emergency placements, permitting a placement with a relative or friend of the child in a household not approved for a period of up to six weeks, where the authority have interviewed the prospective foster-parents' household and obtained an undertaking from them to carry out duties specified in the regulation.

There is provision in reg. 10 for the restriction of placements outside England and Wales. Reg. 12 deals with termination of fostering placements.

Under reg. 12, registers must be kept in confidence by the authorities, of placements, and of foster-parents. Regulations 13 to 16 deal with case records of children in foster placements. Records must also be kept under reg. 14 in relation to foster-parents. Certain documents and information must form part of the case records, and these are listed in reg. 13, including reports of visits and interviews; placement undertakings and agreements; emergency undertakings; placement notices; and information relating to the child's background, health and development which is considered relevant. For foster-parents, the record must include approval notices; review reports; and records of each placement with that person (including notes as to each).

The records must be kept for a period of 75 years from the child's birth, or 15 years from the child's death, if he or she dies before reaching majority (reg. 15).

Inter-agency cooperation is vital in child care, and reg. 16 seeks to formally encourage this. Practitioners may find the booklet *Working Together*, published by HMSO in 1988 (at £4.90), useful reading.

Regulation 17 sets out arrangements for supervision of

placements by area authorities on behalf of another authority.

Regulation 18 protects the child who is placed by a voluntary organisation, ensuring that the local authority for the area has the power to oversee the placement and visit the child in the home in which he or she is placed, with power to remove the child if necessary.

Regulation 19 contains transitional provisions.

Magistrates' Courts (Custodianship Orders) (Amendment) Rules 1989

(SI 1989, No. 383)

Came into force 1 April 1989
These rules amend the Magistrates' Courts (Custodianship Orders) Rules 1985 (SI 1985 No. 1695), introducing additions and amendments to rr. 4, 5 and 6.

A magistrates' court has power, when dealing with an application for custody, adoption or access in relation to a child made under the Guardianship of Minors Act 1971, or under the Domestic Proceedings and Magistrates' Courts Act 1978, to treat that application as an application for custodianship under the Children Act 1975, s.33. When doing so, the court may 'name' a specified person as the applicant for custodianship. If it does so, that person will no longer have to supply a medical report on the child's health to the court. The court also has the power to make certain named categories of people defendants in the custodianship application. Those people include the child's parent(s) or guardian; the local authority in whose care the child is placed; any voluntary organisation with parental rights in respect of the child; anyone liable to maintain the child under a court order or agreement; or anyone with actual or legal custody of the child.

The final amendment is in relation to illegitimacy. The Family Law Reform Act 1987 goes some way towards removing the remnants of the social stigma of illegitimacy and these rules follow that lead. For further discussion on the provisions relating to the Family Law Reform Act, 1987 and ancillary amendments, please see below on the Family Law Reform Act 1987 (Commencement No. 2) Order 1989 (SI 1989 No. 382).

Family Law Reform Act 1987 (Commencement No. 2) Order 1989

(SI 1989 No. 382)

Came into force 1 April 1989
This order implements most of the provisions of the Family Law Reform Act 1987 which are not yet in force. The main part of the Act came into force on 4 April 1988 (under the Family Law Reform Act 1987 (Commencement No. 1) Order 1988 (SI 1988 No. 425)). This order implements the remaining sections as from 1 April 1989, with the exception of ss. 9, 23, 32 and paras 21 to 25 of sch. 2. These last few provisions remain outstanding.

Together with this commencement order come subsidiary amendments to the Magistrates' Court Rules in the Magistrates' Courts (Family Law Reform Act 1987) (Miscellaneous Amendments) Rules 1989 (SI 1989 No. 384) and also to the County Court Rules in the County Court (Amendment No. 2) Rules 1989 (SI 1989 No. 381). The effect of these provisions is discussed in Home Ofice Circular 24/1989.

Note that parts of the Family Law Reform Act 1987 will be repealed when the Children Act 1989 is implemented. The relevant provisions of the Children Act 1989 are discussed in chapter 1.

Basically, the intention behind the Family Law Reform Act 1987 was stated in s.1 of the Act to construe statutory references to certain relationships, e.g., those between parents and children, without regard to whether the child's mother and father were married to each other at given times. In other words, it attempts to minimise the stigma and social or statutory penalties of illegitimacy. The new way of looking at relationships is to be applied to the provisions of the National Assistance Act 1948 and the Social Security Act 1986, the Family Law Reform Act 1969, the Guardianship of Minors Act 1971, the Guardianship Act 1973, the Children Act 1975 and the Child Care Act 1980. Many of the provisions affected by the 1987 Act relate to maintenance of a child, to parental rights, and, in the case of the Children Act 1975, to custodianship.

The part being now brought into force deals with the rights and duties of parents, and with financial provision for illegitimate children.

The Family Law Reform Act 1987 makes radical changes to financial relief for the children of unmarried parents. The Affiliation Proceedings Act 1957 is repealed, and so a mother seeking financial relief for her child will have to apply under the Guardianship of Minors Act 1971. She will no longer have to prove to the court that she was a 'single woman' at the time of the birth, and she will not be restricted by time-limits in applying for financial relief after the birth of the child. A father may also apply for financial relief against the mother of a child and it will make no difference to the court whether or not the parents of the child were (or are) married to each other. The application of the Guardianship of Minors Act 1971 means that, now, financial relief will be available to a child over the age of 18 in certain circumstances where it was not available under the old affiliation proceedings legislation. As a matter of interest, this benefit, too, is continued in the Children Act 1989, as are the criteria for the making of orders for financial relief under s.12A. Family Law Reform Act 1987, s.12, adds ss.11B to 11D to the Guardianship of Minors Act 1971 making additional provisions for financial relief. Much of this is reflected in the Children Act 1989 as are the provisions for the recognition of maintenance agreements between unmarried parents as having valid contractual status, and capable of alteration or variation by the courts.

These proceedings are now under the Guardianship Acts and so an appeal lies to the High Court, and no longer to the Crown Court. This is reflected in the provisions of the Children Act 1989 (when implemented) where appeal against care and supervision decisions in a magistrates' court will lie to the High Court, rather than to the Crown Court as before.

Amendments are made to the Births and Deaths Registration Act 1953 by the Family Law Reform Act 1987, s.24. A natural father may become a 'qualified informant' for the purpose of registration of the birth of his child, and may be registered as the father if he has an order for parental rights in his favour under the Family Law Reform Act 1987, and agrees that he is the father of the child; or if he is responsible physically or financially for the child under the provisions of s.9 or s.11B of the Guardianship of Minors Act 1971.

A putative father of a child (i.e., one not married to the mother of a child at the time of the child's birth) may apply to the court for an order that he be given parental rights and duties in respect of that child. The natural father, therefore, is now able to acquire through court proceedings equal rights with the child's mother, and to share those rights with the mother in the same way as if he were married to the mother. He could also share those rights with a lawfully appointed guardian of the child. The courts able to grant such an order are a magistrates' court, a county court and the High Court. Under the Children Act 1989 (when implemented), the father of a child may acquire parental responsibility, not only by court order, but also by agreement with the mother of the child. The effect of the potential acquisition of parental rights by putative fathers is to enable them, having acquired those rights, to have the power to give or withold consent to adoption of the child; to become or appoint a guardian of the child; and to resolve disputes over matters such as custody with the child's mother through applications to the courts under the Guardianship of Minors Act 1971 and the Guardianship Act 1973.

A father with parental rights will at present become a potential party to care proceedings relating to the child under the Children and Young Persons Act 1969; and may therefore apply for the discharge of a care order relating to the child. Such a father may also represent the child in care proceedings or, alternatively, he may be entitled to legal aid in his own right where there is a conflict of interest with the child and therefore a separate representation order is made by the court. When the Children Act 1989 is in force, a father with parental responsibilities will have specific rights under that Act, see chapter 1.

The Magistrates' Courts (Family Law Reform Act) (Miscellaneous Amendments) Rules 1989 simply make amendments bringing the present rules into line with the new provisions by making the references relate to the terms used in the Family Law Reform Act 1987.

The Magistrates' Courts (Custodianship Orders) (Amendment) Rules 1989 fulfil the same function of relating the existing rules to the new provisions, and also make an additional change. Formerly, when a court decided to treat an application for adoption or an application under Guardianship of Minors Act 1971, s.9, as an application for custodianship, the local authority had to become a defendant in the case. This rule is abolished. Also, a person who was treated by the court as an applicant under r.4 need no longer have to supply the court with a medical report dealing with the child's state of health.

Legal Aid Act 1988 (Commencement No. 3) Order 1989

(SI 1989 No. 288)

Came into force 1 April 1989
This order brought into force from 1 April 1989 most of the Legal Aid Act 1988.

Legal aid is available for the types of case listed in sch.2 to the Act.

Referring specifically to family cases, the cost of legal representation in proceedings in a magistrates' court, county court, the High Court, Court of Appeal and House of Lords will be met by the Legal Aid Board, subject to means. The position is very much the same as it was under the Legal Aid Act 1974, but there are some changes in legal aid in cases relating to children. Family proceedings are of course included in the list of proceedings in which legal aid is available.

These cases include those brought under the Guardianship of Minors Act 1971 and the Guardianship Act 1973; custodianship matters brought under the Children Act 1975, Part II; proceedings under Part I of the Domestic Proceedings and Magistrates' Courts Act 1978; proceedings in relation to an application for leave of the court to remove a child from a person's custody under s.27 or s.28 of the Adoption Act 1976, or proceedings in which the making of an order under Part II or s.29 or s.55 of the Adoption Act 1976 is opposed by any party to the proceedings. The schedule also includes maintenance proceedings brought under the National Assistance Act 1948, the Maintenance Orders Act 1950, and the Maintenance Orders Act 1958, or the Supplementary Benefits Act 1976, together with maintenance enforcement proceedings in relation to orders made abroad under the Maintenance Orders (Reciprocal Enforcement) Act 1972.

Part VI of the Act defines the care proceedings in which legal aid is available, and now includes proceedings under Part IA and ss.3, 5 and 67(2) of the Child Care Act 1980. Sections 27 and 28 deal with the scope and availability of legal aid in care cases, but must be read in conjunction with the Legal Aid in Criminal and Care Proceedings

(General) Regulations 1989 and the Legal Aid in Criminal Care Proceedings (Costs) Regulations 1989, both of which are discussed above.

Affiliation proceedings in a magistrates' court or the Crown Court under the Affiliation Proceedings Act 1957 were included in sch. 2 until the repeal of the Affiliation Proceedings Act 1957 by the Family Law Reform Act 1987. Schedule 7, para. 11 took effect on 1 April 1989. Since that date, applications for financial relief in respect of illegitimate children are to be brought under the Guardianship of Minors Act 1971, as amended.

Access to Personal Files (Social Services) Regulations 1989

(SI 1989 No. 206)

Came into force 1 April 1989
These regulations brought into force on 1 April 1989 the Access to Personal Files Act 1987.

The Social Services department of any local authority is obliged to provide, in response to a written enquiry, access to personal information about the person asking for disclosure. Payment of a fee of up to £10 may be requested by the social services department. 'Personal information' includes information and opinions relating to that person. There are some exceptions to the provisions for the disclosure, which are that where disclosure would be likely to cause serious harm to the physical or mental health of the person requesting it or anyone else, the local authority will only have to disclose so much of the information held as will not cause such harm.

Where disclosure would be likely to reveal the identity of a person to whom the information relates or who has provided information (other than the identity of a health professional or social services employee employed to provide such information) and the person(s) affected have not consented to the disclosure of their identity, then, again, the local authority only have to disclose so much of the information as they can without giving away that person's identity.

There are other exceptions, which are that disclosure need not be made where it would prejudice the prevention or detection of crime, or the apprehension or prosecution of offenders; where the information is contained in a report made for the juvenile court and may be witheld from the person enquiring; where disclosure is not permitted under existing adoption rules; and where the information is covered by the rules of legal professional privilege. Where a person has had access to information, and considers it to be factually wrong, then notice may be given to the local authority to rectify their records. The regulations include provision for complaint about denial of access to information, or refusal to rectify erroneous material. There is a time-limit of 28 days during which the complainant may request a review of the matter by a committee of three local authority members.

It remains to be seen how open the local authorities will be to applications for access to information. It seems that there are so many exceptions in the regulations that where a local authority are determined to block access to certain information, it would be potentially possible to do so, and since the appeal for a review lies to three local authority members, it may well be that changes to an original decision may be difficult to obtain. It is hoped that local authorities will act within the spirit of the legislation. Certainly, freer access to information should enhance trust and encourage a better working relationship with clients and the social services departments of local authorities.

3

CASES

Brewer v Brewer
The Times, 17 February 1989

Court of Appeal (Purchas and Dillon LJJ)

Subject matter: Breach of matrimonial injunction – appropriate sentence

The marriage of Gwendolyne and Robert Brewer had broken down. On 17 November 1988, His Honour Judge Hewitt, having heard about incidents of violence by Robert Brewer which included threats to his wife with a knife, and the firing of an air rifle, made an order forbidding Robert Brewer to use any violence towards his wife or to assault her; and forbidding him to molest her in any way or to cause or encourage anyone else to do the same; and further, after noon on 16 December he should not thereafter reside in the former matrimonial home without the permission of his wife, nor should he enter or remain in the matrimonial home or any part of it without her permission.

In the next month, Robert Brewer began to vacate the matrimonial home, moving out his possessions, and, during this time, his wife stayed away, living with her parents, concerned for her safety. Mrs Brewer applied to the court in January 1989 for a committal order for breach of the orders of 17 November, alleging that Mr Brewer had committed many acts of damage to the matrimonial home and to the property of Mrs Brewer. Before leaving by 16 December, he had removed the electric sockets in the kitchen, and the wiring of the burglar alarm. He had allegedly come back and broken into the house on 22 December, and pulled the video out of its socket, damaged a lamp, and thrown Mrs Brewer's clothes out of the wardrobe. He was also alleged to have broken a window at Mrs

Brewer's daughter's house, threatened Mrs Brewer in public, and to have cut a telephone wire at the home of Mrs Brewer's parents whilst she was living with them. The application for a committal order was heard by Her Honour Judge Paling in the Sunderland County Court on 7 January 1989. The Judge found seven breaches of the earlier injunctions. There was no sense of contrition on the part of Mr Brewer. He expressed no apology to the court for his behaviour. He seemed unable to accept that the marriage had broken down. The Judge committed him to prison for two months for contempt of court. He appealed against the sentence on two grounds:

(a) that the findings of the judge were not supported by the evidence;
(b) the sentence was excessive, and if the committal order were valid, the sentence should have been suspended.

Held
Where there is a first breach of a matrimonial injunction, the appropriate sentence is the imposition of a suspended custodial sentence. Only in exceptional circumstances would an immediate custodial sentence be imposed for first breach. However, in this case, an immediate custodial sentence was merited. The appeal was dismissed, with costs.

R v North Yorkshire County Council, ex parte M
The Times, 20 January 1989

Queen's Bench Division (Ewbank J)

Subject matter: Judicial review of local authority's decision on adoption placement

This was a case where a local authority had a child in their care under a care order, and wished to place that child for adoption. The parents of the child had applied to the juvenile court for discharge of the care order, and that application had been unsuccessful.

The parents then applied to the Queen's Bench Division for judicial review of the local authority's decision to place the child for adoption, arguing that the decision was seriously flawed because the local authority had not asked the guardian *ad litem* appointed by the juvenile court in the proceedings for discharge of the care order to give her opinion on the matter, before reaching their decision to place the child for adoption.

The case came up before Ewbank J, who, having begun the hearing in September 1988, adjourned the case until 16 January 1989 for the final adjudication.

In the intervening period, the local authority had invited the guardian *ad litem* to a meeting at which she had been able to give her opinion, but she had been refused permission to be heard by the adoption panel, although the panel had agreed to read her written report and consider it before making its decision.

Held

There is no provision in the Adoption Agencies Regulations 1983 (SI 1983 No. 1964) for the hearing of oral representations by a guardian *ad litem* appointed by the juvenile court in care proceedings when considering placement of a child for adoption. It seems that the panel has a discretion to request or to hear such oral representations, or not, as it wishes.

It had been suggested that the court should, in this case, make the child a ward of court of it own motion. The High Court has an inherent jurisdiction to exercise such a power, in exceptional circumstances. This would be justifiable where the welfare of the child (the paramount consideration for the High Court) demands it; or where the local authority had behaved so unreasonably that the child's welfare had been adversely affected. Ewbank J reviewed the authorities on the point, and decided that in this case the circumstances were not 'exceptional' within the category enabling the High Court to interfere with the local authority's exercise of their powers. It is interesting to see that the High Court was fairly reluctant in this case to use its wardship jurisdiction to interfere with the power of the local authority. This reluctance is reflected by current legislation in the provisions of the Children Act 1989 under which the High Court is no longer empowered to use its wardship jurisdiction to place a child in the care of a local authority, and the power of a local authority to apply to the High Court to use its inherent jurisdiction in its favour is severely curtailed.

Re G
The Times, 6 February 1989, PCLJ, vol. 2, No. 3, p.41

Court of Appeal (O'Connor LJ and Booth J)

Subject matter: Access – powers of the courts

The child in question was living with her mother, under a county court order made in divorce proceedings, which gave the child's father reasonable access. After problems at home, the child was taken into care by the local authority, who then, having placed the child with foster-parents, commenced care proceedings under the Children and Young Persons Act 1969. Father agreed to the application of the local authority, and supported it, apparently thinking (mistakenly) that the juvenile court could regulate access. Whilst a county court can regulate access under the powers of the Matrimonial Causes Act 1973, s.43(5), the juvenile court at present has no power to do so in care proceedings under the 1969 Act. It is only when access is terminated that an application may be made to the court under the Child Care Act 1980, and this will remain until the relevant provisions in the Children Act 1989, as to access to children in care, are implemented.

The local authority reduced the father's access, and he felt that his relationship with the child was being threatened. He applied to the county court for custody of the child, and for an interim care order to be made under the Matrimonial Causes Act 1973, together with defined access. He failed in his application, and appealed to the Court of Appeal.

Held
The decision of the county court should be upheld. The father's ignorance of the law was not sufficient to vitiate the care order under the 1969 Act. Whilst there was a power for the county court to make a care order under the Matrimonial Causes Act 1973, s.43; in this case the application had been made to the juvenile court under the 1969 Act; and in these circumstances, it was perfectly proper for the juvenile court to make a care order on the application of the local authority whilst the matrimonial county court order was in force. The matrimonial court order for custody would not be effective whilst the care order was in force, but if the care order

were to be discharged, then the custody order would come into effect again. The county court was, however, precluded from making any further care order whilst the first (made in the juvenile court) remained in force.

The proper course of action for the father in these circumstances was to apply to the county court for custody (but not, as he had done, for an interim care order); and then if he were successful in the county court application, he could apply to the juvenile court for a discharge of the care order. He also had redress for termination of access by the local authority by applying to the juvenile court within a specified time-limit after access is terminated, under Child Care Act 1980, s.12 C(2).

This situation is not a satisfactory one, because the Child Care Act 1980 provisions apply where access is terminated, but where, as in this case, it is merely reduced, there is no redress at present in repect of proceedings under the 1969 Act. Also, it seems unfortunate that, in order to obtain fuller access, the father would first have to obtain an order for custody in the county court, and then satisfy the juvenile court that the care order should be discharged, which is quite a difficult task; and that perhaps the discharge of the care order (an order which in this particular case was originally supported by the father) may not have been appropriate.

It may be of use in other cases concerning access in other courts, to note that the Supreme Court Act 1981, s.18(1), does not allow an appeal to the Court of Appeal without leave of the court or tribunal in question, or leave of the Court of Appeal, unless the matter is one where the liberty of the subject is in question, or the custody, education, or welfare of a minor is concerned; or where an applicant for access to a minor is refused all access to that minor. The county court, under the County Court Appeals Order 1981 (SI 1981, No. 1749), however, can hear an appeal relating to access not only where it is refused altogether, but also when it is simply curtailed. This apparent anomaly is because the empowering legislation is worded differently. The sooner that these differences in powers between courts are removed, by the creation of one family court with a framework of coherent and cohesive legislation, the better for all concerned in working within the law relating to children.

Note that the Children Act 1989 creates 'the court' which comprises the High Court, county court and magistrates' court, but the 'family court' with its tier system is yet to come into being. The Children Act 1989 provisions, when implemented, resolve the difficulty of jurisdiction that arose for the father in this particular case, by allowing 'the court' to regulate access to a child in care, and, by creating a unified jurisdiction within 'the court', also resolving the anomaly described above.

Re W (A Minor)
[1989] Fam Law 112, PCLJ, vol. 2 No. 4, p.57

Queen's Bench Division

Subject matter: Access

W was born in December 1985. His parents had not married, and the relationship had broken up before his birth. Mother had found another partner, and had formed a close attachment to him. They intended to marry. Mother was living at her parents' home, and took the baby to live there with her. Her new partner became a frequent visitor, and clearly became attached to the new baby. The baby's natural father, however, took an interest in W at the time of his birth, and during one period of about two months, visited him quite often. When W was about six months old, mother refused to allow the baby's father to see him any more. Father applied for access under the Guardianship of Minors Act 1971, and the court ordered that he should see the baby once every two weeks.

The magistrates gave as their reason for the decision that a child has an interest in having access to both its natural parents; the father was not an unfit person to have access; and that mother had unreasonably refused access because she wanted to encourage the relationship with her new partner. Mother appealed against the decision. During the wait for the appeal to be heard, the mother had married, and was by now living with the baby and her husband in a home of their own. The baby was by now almost three years old.

Held
The welfare of the child is of primary importance, and therefore the courts must look at the child's needs. The court felt that the natural father was a fit person to have access to the baby, but that access in this case would have the effect of causing disruption for the child, who was adapting to his new household. Physical and emotional

stability are important to a child, and therefore in this case the needs of the child must outweigh the wishes of his natural father. The application for access was therefore dismissed. The High Court did not remit the case back to the magistrates court, because time was considered to be important. The High Court substituted its own decision for that of the magistrates and dismissed the application.

Sadiq v Chief Adjudication Officer
[1989] Fam Law 65, PCLJ, vol. 2, No. 5, p.69

Court of Appeal (Slade, Glidewell and Russell LJJ)

Subject matter: Child benefit claims – declarations

Mohammed Sadiq married in 1957, and there are now seven children of the family. The family lived in the United Kingdom until 1974, when they all went to Pakistan. In September 1977, Mr Sadiq returned to the United Kingdom with one son, and in December 1981 another son came to join them.

It was the family plan that when the older child's education in Urdu was completed, the family should all live together in the United Kingdom.

Between 28 December 1981 and 14 October 1984, Mohammed Sadiq claimed one-parent benefit in respect of the two children living with him.

In 1984, Mrs Sadiq and the remaining children joined the family in the UK. The father then claimed child benefit for all the children then resident with him.

The DHSS demanded repayment of the benefit paid to the father in respect of the two children with him from December 1981 to October 1984, on the basis that he had not stated clearly to the DHSS that the separation from his wife was not intended to be permanent. He had in fact failed to answer the relevant question on the application form. The DHSS adjudication officer ordered full repayment of the benefit paid to the father. The father appealed.

Held
Whilst there was no question of bad faith on the part of Mr Sadiq, he was under a duty to exercise due diligence in claiming the benefit, and he had not disclosed a material fact of importance to the claim. He should have realised that his failure to disclose whether his

separation was intended to be permanent or not was vital to the claim he made, and so when payment was made to him by the DHSS it was made in error as a result of a mistake of fact, and should be repaid.

Note
At the time that this case arose, the Social Security Act 1975, s.119(1) and (2) was in force. This provision has now been replaced by the Social Security Act 1986, s.53. The new provision provides in essence, that where it it determined that, whether fraudulently or otherwise, any person has misrepresented, or failed to disclose, a material fact and in consequence of that misrepresentation or failure, a payment has been made in respect of a benefit to which the section applies, or a sum recoverable by the Secretary of State in connection with such payment has not been recovered, then the Secretary of State shall be entitled to recover the amount of any payment which he would not have made, or sum which he would have received but for that misrepresentation or failure to disclose.

In the circumstances of this case, then, it is likely that the finding and order of the court would still have been the same under the new provisions.

Re P (A Minor)
[1989] 1 FLR 182, PCLJ, vol. 2, no. 5, p.74

High Court (Family Division) (Eastham J)

Subject matter: Sterilisation of mentally handicapped girl

P is a mentally handicapped girl. At the time of the case she was 17 years old and, although appearing otherwise normal, had a mental age of approximately six years.

There had been evidence that the girl's mental age would remain at around the age of six but that her general emotional awareness, self-care skills, and social skills would slowly improve, dependant on the quality of care she was receiving at the time.

Her mother foresaw considerable difficulty with her because the girl had the normal sexual urges of any 17-year-old, and would want to be sexually active. She was fast reaching maturity, and soon would be leaving home during the day to attend an adult training centre, with the possibility of later going to live in a residential establishment. She had tried using certain contraceptives, but had experienced unpleasant side-effects. Mother was worried that if the girl became pregnant, she would be quite unable to cope with looking after her baby, that this would inevitably lead to any baby being born to her being taken away from her, and that if this were to happen, it would in all probability be harmful psychologically to the girl. The only way out of this dilemma would be for mother to look after any baby born to P, together with P herself, in one household; and although mother would in theory be willing to do this, it would not be likely to be successful or happy, because of the potential emotional problems that would be caused by the advent of a baby within the existing close relationship between mother and daughter. It was said by the mother that P would be likely to resent the mother giving attention to a baby.

Mother decided to try to resolve the problem by making P a ward of court, and asking the court to give leave for her sterilisation. Medical evidence was adduced as to P's mental capacity, and also as to the likelihood of her being able to cope with a baby on her own. It was accepted that P could not cope with a baby on her own, and that the potential trauma of allowing her to have a baby and then taking it away was one to be avoided. The court considered the potential effect of an abortion on P, should she become pregnant. It was felt that she probably would not understand what the operation was all about.

The court had then to consider whether P could herself consent to sterilisation. To do so, she would have to understand what it was, and the implications of such an operation. Mother wanted the operation to be carried out whilst P was still under 18, whilst the Official Solicitor wanted to wait until the girl was more mature and, impliedly, the danger of pregnancy was more imminent. It was accepted, however, that sterilisation would ultimately be the most likely way of meeting P's needs in the future, if and when she showed that she wanted to have sexual relationships.

The court had to consider the past authorities, and in particular *Re B (A Minor)* (Wardship: *Sterilisation*) [1988] AC 199, in which the House of Lords authorised sterilisation in a case where the girl in question was 17 years old, but had a mental age of a five or six-year-old. The House of Lords had found that the girl could never (however chronologically old she became) reach sufficient metal capacity to consent to the operation herself. The court reiterated that the paramount consideration is the welfare of the ward of court. Here, in this case, medical opinion varied as to whether P could gain sufficient mental capacity to give her own consent to the operation, later in life.

The court heard that the surgeon who would perform the operation (of sterilisation with clips applied bi-laterally over each fallopian tube through a small incision in the region of the navel) could do it in such a way that there would be a high chance of a successful reversal of the sterilisation later in P's life if the need arose. Reversal would be by means of micro-surgery. The chance of success in reversal was put as high as 95%.

In the case of *Re B (A Minor)* above, the question of reversal was not considered in 1987, but is now a very relevant factor to be taken into account. The court was also referred to the judgment of Bush J in *Re M (A Minor) (Wardship: Sterilisation)* [1988] 2 FLR 497 in which a university professor had referred in the case to possible reversal of this type of sterilisation and stated that he regarded the operation as more that of contraception than one of sterilisation, carrying all its concomitant emotive feelings.

Held
In these circumstances, particularly bearing in mind that the operation could in all probability be reversed if P so wished later in her life, the proposed operation for sterilisation should be authorised, and the wardship should be continued.

Re C (A Minor)
The Times, 21 April 1989, PCLJ, vol. 2, No. 5, p. 76

Court of Appeal (Lord Donaldson MR, Lord Balcombe and Nicholls LJ)

Subject matter: Medical treatment of terminally ill child

This case was one which must have been very difficult indeed for the court. A baby girl was born, prematurely, and with an unusually serious form of hydrocephalus which had led to severe brain damage, and which would ultimately cause her early death. The local authority social services department had already made the baby a ward of court, and the High Court had authorised an operation to insert a 'shunt' valve to relieve pressure on the baby's brain. The baby then developed intestinal problems, and the matter came back before the court to decide whether further medical treatment should be given to a child who was already terminally ill. The court had to consider the proposal that this child should have the treatment which any non-handicapped child would receive, and also the need to alleviate the child's suffering, considered together with the awareness that certain treatments could prolong the child's life, but only for a short period, because she was terminally ill. The court heard from a paediatrician that treatment should be aimed at easing suffering rather than short-term prolongation of life, and the judge at first instance agreed with this view.

The original wording of the judge's order was to give leave to the hospital 'to treat the ward to die' and this wording was unfortunate in that it had appeared to authorise the death of the ward. Ward J had revised and amended the wording of the order, changing the words above quoted to 'to allow her life to come to an end peacefully'.

The order made by Ward J also contained the following wording in para. 3, based on his understanding of the paediatrician's report:

> the hospital authority shall administer such treatment to the minor as might relieve her from pain, suffering and distress, *inter alia*, by sedation, but it shall not be necessary either to:
> (a) prescribe and administer antibiotics to treat serious infection, or
> (b) to set up intravenous fusions or nasal gastric feeding regimes.

The Official Solicitor appealed the decision to the Court of Appeal.

Held
That the words in para. 3 of the order of Ward J be deleted, because they appeared to be inconsistent in that they directed the hospital to act so as to relieve the child's pain, suffering and distress, yet they also appeared to preclude the giving of specialist treatment, even though the effect of such specialist treatment could be to achieve that first objective. The Court of Appeal ordered that the advice of the paediatrician be followed, which was that if the child's nurses thought that certain treatments (whether specialist treatments or not), would alleviate the child's suffering, then they should be

considered, but that these specialist treatments should not be given simply because the child developed a serious infection.

Lord Donaldson MR, in the Court of Appeal, made it quite clear that the High Court would not and did not authorise anyone to bring about the death of its ward, and that the judgment as amended was not intended to have this effect.

Incidentally, the Court of Appeal held that this case was one where the issues were of sufficient public importance and interest that, whilst protecting individual privacy, the court should give its decisions and the reasons for those decisions, together with a summary of the relevant facts, and the matters taken into account in reaching those decisions, in open court.

R v Lancashire County Council, ex parte Moore (a Minor)
The Times, 27 March 1989, [1989] 2 FLR 279

Court of Appeal (O'Connor, Croom-Johnson and Balcombe LJJ)

Subject matter: Special educational needs – intensive speech therapy

The Lancashire Education Authority assessed M, a nine year old boy, as having 'special educational needs' within the meaning of the Education Act 1944 (as amended by the Education Act 1981) s.1(1). It was common ground that M suffered from a congenital hearing problem and also a speech deformity, together with a language learning difficulty. It was agreed that he had special educational needs requiring special educational provision, and that he needed intensive speech therapy.

Under the Education Act 1981, once it is established that a child has special educational needs, the local education authority is obliged to make a statement of those needs, and if the 'statement' specifies that special educational provision is necessary, then under the Education Reform Act 1988, sch. 12, para. 83, it must be provided by the local education authority unless the parents of the child have already made arrangements to meet that need.

In this case, the 'statement' was divided into five parts, an introduction followed by Part II dealing with special educational needs; Part III with special educational provision; Part IV with appropriate school and other arrangements; and Part V with non-educational needs and provision. The necessity for speech therapy was mentioned by implication in Part II and directly in Part III. Part IV referred to attendance at the unit for children with language disorders, and Part V was left blank.

The statement was amended and revised, more than once, ending up with Part II as revised and Part III referring directly to the need for access to individual speech therapy on a regular sessional basis; and Part V now no longer blank, but including a recommendation made by an educational psychologist that speech therapy be provided (as a non-educational provision).

The proposal of the education authority in Part V was that he should have 30 minutes' speech therapy each week. This was the normal length of one session, and therefore the boy was effectively being offered one normal-length session per week. In the past he had received more intensive therapy, i.e. individual speech therapy four times each week and also small group language work.

Mother thought that the current proposal for once weekly sessions was insufficient to meet his needs. She tried to persuade the council to increase the therapy provided, but without success. The local authority maintained that the inclusion of the therapy in Part III was an oversight, and that, being a non-educational provision, they were under no duty to provide it. Finally, the child's mother applied for judicial review of the education authority's decision.

The Divisional Court of the Queen's Bench Division held that speech therapy could be a special need within the meaning of the Education Act 1981, s.5(1), despite the protestations of the Lancashire County Council that it was not. The council had argued that the statement in Part III relating to speech therapy as a special educational need had been made in error, was therefore legally unenforceable, and that the local authority was not bound by it at all.

The council appealed to the Court of Appeal.

Held
The Divisional Court's judgment should be upheld. The court implied, *inter alia*, that teaching a child to speak is as much a part of his or her education as teaching communication by writing. Speech therapy was correctly stated as an educational need; and the local education authority was under a duty, therefore, to provide speech therapy. It had also been argued for the council that those who offered speech therapy were not local authority employees, and

that therefore the Education Act 1981 could not have contemplated the inclusion of a facility outside local authority control. The Court of Appeal was unimpressed by this argument, holding that if those who provide speech therapy are not local authority employees, this makes no difference to the duty to provide the therapy required. Reference was made to the findings of the Committee of Enquiry into the Education of Handicapped Children and Young People (The Warnock Report, 1978 Cmnd 7212) and to the White Paper – Special Needs in Education (1980 Cmnd 7996). Note, too, the Education (Special Educational Needs) Regulations 1983 (SI 1983 No. 29) which give effect to certain provisions of the Education Act 1981, and also deal with the advice which should be sought by a local education authority for the purpose of an assessment.

The decision of the Divisional Court that speech therapy could be special educational provision within the Education Act 1981, s.5(1), was properly made. So long as there is a reference in Part III of the statement to 'access to individual speech therapy on an intensive basis' the council is under a duty to provide such therapy. The mistake of the council, if any, was the inclusion of a reference to it again in Part V. The reference to it in Part V can be ignored.

Waterman v Waterman
[1989] 1 FLR 380, PCLJ, vol. 2, No. 7, p.104

Court of Appeal (Sir Stephen Brown P, Croom-Johnson and Taylor LJJ)

Subject matter: Periodical payments – duration

Mr and Mrs Waterman had been married for 17 months. Before marrying, they had lived together for a similar period. They had a child, who, at the time of the case, was five years old.

Pursuant to divorce proceedings, Mrs Waterman was awarded custody of the child. She applied for maintenance for herself and the child. Her former husband was ordered to pay maintenance by way of periodical payments for the child until the child reached the age of 17; and to pay a lump sum to his former wife, together with periodical payments for a five-year period. Hutchinson J, at first instance directed that Mrs Waterman could not apply for an extension of that period after the expiration of five years.

Although the judge had power under Matrimonial Causes Act 1973, s.28(1A) (as amended), to make such a direction, and it was presumably made because the wife had a potential means of earning her own income which she could more easily undertake in five years' time when the child in question would be 10 years old; nevertheless, Mrs Waterman thought the order to be unfair. It was argued on her behalf that she could not anticipate her situation in five years' time, and that it would be most unfair to her to restrict her power to apply for an extension of the period during which payments should be made.

Hutchinson J had taken into account that Mrs Waterman had been employed as a secretary before her marriage, and that she had undergone a training course since the divorce which would enhance her skills (and presumably, her chances of gaining employment); but it was argued for Mrs Waterman on appeal that he did not give sufficient weight to the fact that she had a young child to look after.

Hutchinson J refused leave to appeal, and Mrs Waterman applied to the Court of Appeal for leave to appeal against the order.

Held

There is no appeal in relation to the lump-sum payment, nor as to the quantum of the periodical payments. However, leave to appeal was granted in respect of the order for payments to Mrs Waterman to terminate after five years, and the direction not to apply for an extension of that period, made under s.28(1A) of the 1973 Act.

The Court of Appeal gave considerable thought to the principle of 'a clean break' as described by Lord Scarman in his speech in *Minton* v *Minton* [1979] AC 593. It was felt that whilst there may be a time after dissolution of a marriage when the party in whose favour an order for financial provision had been made would have to come to terms with financial independence; the situation is different in a case where there is a child or children for whom the parties share a continuing obligation. Sir Stephen Brown P cited the case of *Moore* v *Moore* (1981) 11 Fam Law 109, in which Ormrod J said '. . . in my judgment, the so-called principle of a clean break has no application where there are young children', and went on to observe that the new s.25A imposes a mandatory duty on the court in every case to apply itself to the questions set out in s.25A(2) whenever it decides to make a periodical payments order in favour of a party to the marriage. He added that it may be possible on the facts to recognise a date when the party in whose favour the order is made will be able to adjust without undue hardship to the termination of financial dependence on the other party.

The Court of Appeal found on the facts that it was impossible at that time to predict the date of Mrs Waterman's possible financial independence, given that there was a degree of uncertainty in both her future position and also that of the child. Although admitting some hesitation concerning the five-year period for payments, nevertheless it could not be said that the judge was plainly wrong in coming to that conclusion after a review of all the circumstances; but it was plainly wrong to make an order under s.28(1A) preventing the mother from applying to the court for an extension of that period. This was a Draconian prohibition. The appeal was allowed, the order for termination of payments after five years endorsed, but the direction under s.28(1A) set aside.

Attorney-General's Reference (No. 1 of 1989)
The Times, 1 August 1989, PCLJ, Vol. 2, No. 8, p. 112

Court of Appeal

Subject matter: Sentence for incest – guidelines

The Crown Court imposed a sentence of three years' imprisonment on a man convicted on three counts of incest with his oldest daughter, and one count of indecent assault on a younger daughter. He had begun to commit incest with the older girl when she was 11 years old, and had continued this until she was nearly 16. The Attorney-General felt that the sentence was too lenient, and applied to the Court of Appeal under Criminal Justice Act 1988, s. 36, for a review of that sentence. The Court of Appeal considered all the issues involved, and took the view that it would be helpful if guidelines were laid down as to the level of sentence in incest cases. Lord Lane LCJ therefore laid down the following guidelines.

(a) *In relation to girls over 16.* Generally, from three years' imprisonment to a nominal penalty depending on whether force was used; the degree of harm, if any, to the girl; including the degree of corruption; whether, with an older girl, she had been willing or even the instigator; the desirability, where appropriate, of minimising family disruption.

(b) *In relation to girls aged 13 to 16.* Generally, a sentence between three and five years, with much the same factors as for the 16 and over age group being relevant for consideration by the court, although the likelihood of corruption increased in inverse proportion to the child's age.

(c) *In relation to girls under 13.* Where a girl is just below her 13th birthday, and there are no particularly adverse or favourable features on a guilty plea, the appropriate term of imprisonment is about six years.

Where a girl is younger than this, the younger she is when the sexual approach is commenced, the more likely it is that the father exploited his position due to the girl's dependence and the more likely that the girl's will was overborne. Accordingly, the more serious would be the circumstances.

The Court of Appeal laid down guidelines, too, concerning aggravating factors which, impliedly, would lead to heavier sentences:

(a) physical or psychological damage to the girl,
(b) frequency of occurrence of incest over a long period of time,
(c) violence or the threat of violence, or fear induced,
(d) accompanying perversions abhorrent to the girl, e.g., buggery or fellatio,
(e) pregnancy of the girl because of failure of the father to take contraceptive precautions,
(f) similar offences committed by the defendant against more than one child.

Factors which would mitigate and therefore, impliedly, potentially lessen a sentence:

(a) guilty plea – to be met with an appropriate discount, dependent upon how promptly the accused confessed, and his degree of contrition, etc.;
(b) genuine affection on the part of the defendant rather than an intention to use the girl as an outlet for purely sexual needs,
(c) where the girl had previous sexual experience,
(d) where the girl had made deliberate attempts at seduction,
(e) where, as occasionally occurred, a shorter term of imprisonment for the father was of benefit to both victim and family.

B v *T*
[1989] 2 FLR 31, PCLJ, Vol. 2, No. 8, p.112

Court of Appeal (Mustill and Balcombe LJJ)

Subject matter: Custody – Divisional Court may not substitute own views for future on paper evidence alone

This case came before the Court of Appeal in November 1988. Originally the custody case had been heard by the Warley Magistrates' Court. The magistrates' decision was the subject of appeal by the mother to the Divisional Court (Family Division) where judgment was given by Sir Stephen Brown P; father then took the case to the Court of Appeal.

The circumstances of the case were that, in November 1988, there were two children of the family, a boy, born in July 1985, and a girl, born in January 1987. The parents were not married to each other, but had lived together from September 1983 until January 1988. When they parted, then, their daughter was a year old, and their son just over three years old.

In January 1988, mother left the relationship, and went to live elsewhere, taking the girl with her. She established her new home on the ninth floor of a block of flats. The boy remained with his father, in the house which had been the family home. The parents issued cross summonses in the Warley Magistrates' Court against each other for custody of the children.

One of the issues considered by the magistrates was the respective facilities which could be provided by each parent. Mother had no garden for the children to play in, (the play area being five minutes' walk from her flat) whilst father had a semi-detached house with a garden. Father therefore had more spacious accommodation, and of course, it had been the family home. The magistrates found, however, that the father and mother both had adequate accommodation for the upbringing of the children, and that both, being unemployed, had sufficient time to care for the children.

Father had a car, and also a supportive family network and was considered a fit person to meet the physical and emotional needs of the children.

It was noted by the magistrates that: 'Although a caring mother, the mother is an immature person who could not cope with domestic chores. Often clothes were not washed, and if washed, left

CASES 69

outside on the washing line or around the radiators in the house'. Admittedly this is just a quotation from the stated case, but one wonders what significance the magistrates drew from this. It was, however, also noted that mother had insisted on the boy (who was an active child) having an afternoon sleep, and that she had given him Calpol (which is a paracetamol based medicine for children) to induce sleep. How often this had occurred is unclear. Mother had also been treated for depression, and was found by the magistrates to have 'placed too much emphasis on material goods, rather than the welfare of the family'.

The magistrates court having considered the circumstances, and having the benefit of a welfare report, felt that whilst the mother and father were caring and loving parents; and both could look after the day to day care of the children; the father was the more capable of looking after the children's emotional and physical well-being, and was more able to run a home. Having a car, he could take the children out, and he had the support of his family. Since the court felt that the best interests of the children would be met by keeping them together, it ordered custody of both children to the father, and allowed the mother reasonable access.

Mother appealed to the Divisional Court. The case waited some months before it was heard. There had been a stay, so that in fact the girl remained with her mother, and the boy with his father, during this time.

It was held by the Divisional Court that the magistrates had given insufficient weight to the ages of the children; in particular the little girl, who had lived all her life with her mother. The justices had attached too much weight to material and peripheral matters, and too little attention to the effect of removing young children from the care of their mother. It was ordered that both children should live with mother, with reasonable access to the father.

Incidentally, Sir Stephen Brown P said in the course of giving judgment that 'There is no basis in the evidence, in my judgment, for the implied suggestion that her (the mother) giving the children doses of Calpol was in some way a wrong thing to do'.

Father appealed to the Court of Appeal. Again, there was a stay so that the children did not in fact move during the wait for the final decision.

Held
Having considered all the circumstances fully, that undue weight had been given to the physical and material circumstances of father.

Insufficient weight had been given by the magistrates to the fact that the little girl had always lived with her mother. There was no reference in the justices' reasons to the question whether the mother, on her own, was doing better with the girl than she had with the two children; and there was no trace in the documents before the court of considerations by the justices of the long term future. The Court of Appeal took the view that there was insufficient information available to reach a final decision, and that the only practical course was to remit the case back to the magistrates to explore the issues in greater depth. Although the main part of the Divisional Court's judgment was correct, in that the justices' action could not be maintained; it was not right for the Divisional Court to substitute its own views of what should happen in the future on paper evidence alone.

The Divisional Court's judgment was therefore set aside, and the case sent back to the magistrates for a final decision; making an interim order for custody of the girl to mother and of the boy to father.

The magistrates finally decided that mother should have the custody of both children.

This case could have had the potentially very damaging effect of moving the children between their parents, but because the various courts had granted a stay of execution pending further hearings, the girl had remained with her mother, and the boy with his father during the proceedings. The final move therefore, was only one, for the boy, from his father to his mother.

4

Circulars and Official Publications

Home Office Circular 24/1989

This circular contains much useful information about the provisions of the Family Law Reform Act 1987 which were brought into force on 1 April 1989 by the Family Law Reform Act 1987 (Commencement No. 2) Order 1989 (SI 1989 No. 382). Practitioners will know that the first commencement order in 1988 (SI 1988 No. 425) brought part of the Act into force on 4 April 1988. There have been ancillary amendments to other rules to take account of the implementations, including the Magistrates' Courts (Family Law Reform Act 1987) (Miscellaneous Amendments) Rules 1989 (SI 1989, No. 384); the County Court (Amendment No. 2) Rules 1989 (SI 1989 No. 1687); and the Magistrates' Courts (Custodianship Orders) (Amendment) Rules 1989, which, in addition to making amendments consequential on the Family Law Reform Act 1987, also make two changes to the Magistrates' Courts (Custodianship Orders) Rules 1985.

The circular explains some of the basic changes, and it is well worth obtaining a copy of it. The following summary is for quick reference.

The Affiliation Proceedings Act 1957 is now repealed. With the intention of removing the stigma and disadvantages of illegitimacy, there is no longer a separate and distinct procedure for enforcing financial provision for an illegitimate child. Proceedings will now be under the Guardianship of Minors Act 1971, as amended, as they are for all children, irrespective of whether their parents were married to each other or not. The Guardianship of Minors Act 1971 can be used to obtain financial relief without custody being in issue.

Another intention of the legislation was, it seems, to further the equality of maternal and paternal rights, and to this end, a father may now apply for financial relief against the mother of an illegitimate child.

Other former limitations are removed. A mother need no longer be bound by time-limits after the birth of a child in claiming for financial relief; nor need she have to satisfy the court that she was a 'single woman' at the time of the birth.

Written maintenance agreements may be varied by the courts where they contain an acknowledgment of paternity. It is interesting to see how these provisions lead into those shortly to come into force within the Children Act 1989, see chapter 1.

There are provisions for agreements to be made between parents of a child as to the exercise, but not the transfer, of parental rights. A natural father of a child may apply to the court for an order giving him the same rights and duties in respect of the child as a married father of that child would have had. He may now share the legal rights of a parent of his natural child with the child's mother. Disputes over the children will be resolved by the courts in the same way as disputes between married couples.

The reference in the Children and Young Persons Act 1969 to 'parent' is now amended by Family Law Reform Act 1987, s.8, to include a natural father of a child who has a court order in force giving him actual custody of the child. Section 70 (the interpretation section) of the Children and Young Persons Act 1969 is also amended to take in a new subsection (1A) which provides that the father of an illegitimate child shall be treated as a parent for the purposes of the Act.

The relevance of being treated as 'a parent' under the Act is that the parent is entitled to notice of care proceedings, and to make applications and appeals under the Act in respect of the child. A parent is also liable, in criminal proceedings, to enter into a recognisance on behalf of the child, or for payment of compensation to third parties for offences committed by the child. One of the grounds for care at present is that a child is beyond parental control, and again, a natural father would (in the circumstances outlined above) be included in this concept.

As amended by Family Law Reform Act 1987, s. 8(2) to (5), the Child Care Act 1980 also now includes a father with actual custody of his natural child in the category of 'parent' for various specified purposes, which includes the right to request the return of a child from voluntary care, or to remove a child from voluntary care with

CIRCULARS AND OFFICAL PUBLICATIONS

appropriate notice, and/or to oppose the assumption of parental rights by the local authority.

Note that some parts of the Family Law Reform Act 1987 will not now be brought into force. Sections 9, 24, 25 and 30, and parts of s.33, will remain unused.

The Children Act 1989 Notice of Royal Assent and of the Provisions to Take Early Effect

Local Authority Circular LAC(89)16, Health Notice HN (89)25, Welsh Office Circular WO 62/89
This circular gives notice of the Royal Assent to the Children Act 1989 on 16 November 1989, and introduces certain provisions of the Act which take early effect. It records that the government intends to bring the remainder of the Children Act into force by October 1991.

Hearsay Evidence in Civil Cases Concerning Children
A measure which required urgent implementation was that relating to the admissibility of hearsay evidence in proceedings relating to children. Until recently, the courts were prepared to 'bend the rules' in order to admit hearsay evidence in care matters in the same way that it may be admitted in wardship proceedings. However, in *K v K, The Times,* 9 June 1989, the Court of Appeal ruled that hearsay evidence is only admissible in matrimonial proceedings in accordance with the exceptions laid down in the present law. This ruling meant that in the matrimonial jurisdiction of the county court, potentially valuable evidence could be lost because it would be rendered inadmissible. Children Act 1989, s.96(3), enables the Lord Chancellor to make orders overriding the rules relating to hearsay in civil proceedings in respect of evidence connected with the upbringing, maintenance, or welfare of children. That subsection is in force as from 16 November 1989. However, the orders have not yet been made.

Meaning of 'Parent'
In accordance with the intention of Parliament to give parents equal rights, the Children Act 1989 will ultimately repeal the Child Care Act 1980, replacing it with other provisions. The Family Law Reform Act 1987 had intended to make changes towards equality,

but had omitted to deal with a natural (unmarried) father's right of access to a child in care. Until that takes effect, there are transitional provisions in sch. 12, para. 35, amending the Child Care Act 1980. One amendment is that the word 'parent' will include, in addition to the child's mother or married father, a putative (i.e., unmarried, or natural) father of a child in several provisions, including that relating to the right of a parent to request access to a child in care. This means that a putative father may apply to the court for access to a child of his who is in the care of a local authority if the local authority terminates or refuses access.

'Married' means, in this context, married to the mother of the child at the time of the child's birth.

This provision is now in force since 16 November 1989.

Paternity Blood Tests
Children Act 1989, s.89, makes amendments to the provisions for blood tests to establish paternity in Family Law Reform Act 1969, s.20. It inserts two subsections into s.20, providing that where an application is made for a blood test to establish the paternity of a person under 18, the application shall specify who is to carry out the tests. The court may then direct that the specified person shall carry out the tests, or where the court considers it inappropriate to specify that person, it may decline to give the direction applied for.

This section is in force since 16 November 1989.

Provision for Children with Special Needs
On 17 January 1990, Children Act 1989, sch. 12, came into force, amending the Education Act 1981. It will then enable a local education authority responsible for making statements of special needs under Education Act 1981, s.7, to arrange for any child with special needs in respect of whom they maintain a statement, to attend any establishment outside England and Wales which specialises in providing for such children. Fees or costs may be funded by the local education authority.

CIRCULARS AND OFFICAL PUBLICATIONS

Introduction to the Children Act 1989

HMSO £4.95

Prepared with the help of Jonathan Whybrow, who worked on the Children Bill team, this excellent book contains 90 pages of useful information. It is, as its title implies, an introduction to the Children Act 1989 and sets out the basic principles and provisions of the Act in the context of government thinking and of other legislation.

It pulls together different sections of the Act, relating them to each other, and making sense of much which could otherwise be confusing.

Readable enough for a layman, but detailed enough for practitioners, it is an essential addition to the family lawyer's library.

The introduction does not set out to be a detailed analysis of the Act, but rather is a guide to the basic premises of the provisions and the context in which they were enacted. There are many useful clues to how it is hoped that the courts may implement the provisions when the Act comes into force, and to how the provisions were meant by Parliament to be interpreted. Much of the book reflects government thinking, for example, 'The Act rests on the belief that children are generally best looked after within the family with both parents playing a full part and without resort to legal proceedings'.

The book is divided up into an introductory discussion, followed by sections on parental responsibility, court proceedings, local authority services for children and families, children looked after by local authorities, protection of children at risk, welfare of children away from home, and finally, a section on adoption, procedure, evidence and other matters.

When looking for a specific topic, for example, the effect of court orders, it is often necessary to refer to the contents list at the beginning of the book to discover which section contains the information required, but the list is comprehensive and this proves no great hardship.

The book is clearly written, and will prove invaluable to practitioners.

5

COMMERCIAL PUBLICATIONS

Representing Children: Child Interviews – A Pictorial Aid for Guardians ad Litem and Child Care Panel Solicitors
By D. Clark, Kent and Sussex Independent Counselling Agency, £8.95, 1989

This is a pictorial aid which is designed to assist practitioners (including solicitors and guardians *at litem*) in preparing cases involving children. It is designed to help in communication with children, not an easy task for many, and it offers a very useful new way of approaching a potentially difficult task. Listening effectively to children and really hearing what they are telling you is not only vital to the case, but it is also vital to establishing a good relationship with the child. Maybe it should also be compulsory reading for parents, too!

Law and the Family
By John Dewar, Butterworths, 403pp., £13.95

This is a readable book.

John Dewar, formerly a lecturer in law at the University of Warwick, takes a practical and sensible approach to the issues of family law. He looks at the current social, political and economic attitudes of society and asks a few very telling questions about issues that many of us may well have been setting aside for a while.

The book offers a source of insight into the reasoning of the courts in reaching their decisions, and although it does not set itself up to be a complete work of reference, it offers a useful viewpoint for those who deal with family law cases. It is designed to provide sufficient information for the undergraduate studying family law,

COMMERCIAL PUBLICATIONS

and also was intended to provide a 'way in' to the different ways of thinking and writing about the subject.

It is divided into topics, the first, predictably, being introductory and leading the reader into the possible different ways of looking at the subject generally. There is an introduction to the court system, to the services and facilities available, and a look at the functions of various court officials and employees, including others such as guardians *ad litem*.

The book then goes on to look at the concepts of marriage and cohabitation, defining both these terms and looking at the effects of each. Void and voidable marriages are discussed, and much technical legal information is available in a palatable form. Transsexualism, homosexuality, bigamy and mental handicap are discussed in addition to many other topics including prohibited degrees, polygamy and the attitude of society to women's bodies, reflected in the law relating to abortion and rape.

The chapter on parents and children takes a look at the definition of parenthood and its biological and legal proof. Egg and embryo donation, surrogacy and motherhood are discussed, blood tests, parental rights and duties, and children's rights. Guardianship has a place here.

Income is discussed in different ways. The legal enforceability of maintenance agreements, effects of failure to maintain, factors affecting maintenance and enforcement of orders are all given ample space. There is a very useful section on welfare benefits, often lacking in general textbooks, and there are tables for calculation in the text. There is an explanation for the practitioner or student of the different benefits available.

Property is dealt with from the viewpoint of personal property, then the family home, and followed by the rights of third parties. The effects of death are considered, and problems relating to rented property and homelessness are discussed.

There is a chapter on violence and breakdown of relationships. The author examines the role of the police, civil law, with special reference to injunctions and their effectiveness, and the remedies available under the present legislation.

Divorce and conciliation are examined from the point of view of law and procedure. Money and property in divorce are treated in the same way, in some detail, and with special reference to the guidelines available for financial relief orders, and the way in which the guidelines are applied in practice. Welfare benefit considerations are taken into account.

Children and divorce form the topic for another chapter. Consideration is given to the regulation of post-divorce relationships. There is a full discussion of the alternative orders available in addition to practical considerations.

The chapter on the State as parent looks at care, and the role of local authorities and other organisations. Much of the material here will change when the Children Act 1989 is fully implemented in October 1991, but until then it is useful and relevant. The chapter on social parenthood, custodianship and adoption, again contains much useful and presently relevant information. Adoption law is under review at the present time, and there are some changes to come, but at present the material here is relevant and operative.

There is, too, a chapter on wardship, which provides an introduction to the High Court's wardship jurisdiction, and discusses the proposals for reform. The Children Act 1989 now has carried out reforms, altering the wardship jurisdiction of the High Court, and removing the power of the High Court to exercise its inherent jurisdiction in placing children in the care of local authorities. The only route to care will be through the provisions of the Children Act 1989.

The book finishes with an extensive bibliography.

All in all, a readable, but academic work full of useful information and reference material. Well worth its cost.

Mothers without Custody
By G. Grief and M. Pabst, Lexington Books, US, £7.00

A good deal of attention has been given to the plight and the feelings of fathers who do not have the custody of their children, but little, it seems, to mothers in this situation. It is good to see a book on this subject. Social attitudes, and the pressures put upon women by society, (and by the courts at times), can set up enormous stress. This is a topic which has to be of interest for all who are endeavouring to help in any way those mothers who are, for whatever reason, without custody of their children.

COMMERCIAL PUBLICATIONS 79

Adoption Act Manual
By Richard Jones, Sweet & Maxwell, 263 pp., £18.00

Useful and practical, a reference book for the practitioner's bookshelf. The Adoption Act 1976 came into force on 1 January 1988, and this book sets out to provide relevant information relating to adoption law and practice, in a coherent form.

The book begins with a reproduction of the Adoption Act 1976 in full. It is very useful to have the text of the Act ready for reference. In addition to the text are notes printed in the book below the sections to which they refer. This is an excellent way to provide the relevant information at a glance for the busy practitioner.

The second part of the book deals with dedicated legislation, reproducing the orders and regulations made in relation to adoption, together with the Adoption Rules 1984, and the Magistrates' Courts (Adoption) Rules 1984.

The third section of the book deals with circulars, which are reproduced for reference.

There is a flow chart of the time-limits for making adoption orders, and orders authorising proposed foreign adoptions, simply set out and easy to follow for busy practitioners or for students.

The index is comprehensive.

A useful reference work.

Legal Issues in Human Reproduction
Edited by Sheila McLean, Gower Publishing Group, 239pp.
£14.95 and £25.00

This book looks at the legal issues following on from the advances made in reproductive techniques. The work is written by a group of authors, each of whom has contributed chapters dealing with a wide variety of issues in this field. Abortion, selective treatment of handicapped infants, sterilisation of the mentally handicapped, surrogacy and more. There is a considerable amount of medical detail in the book, which is explained to the lay reader in a clear way, and which does not feel patronising nor confusing in its style. The experience of both the UK and other countries is mentioned in the work, and the result is that the reader is encouraged to think further about the issues discussed, and to look more closely at the results of modern research and development in this area.

This is of general interest to the legal practitioner, and forms part of a series of books by Gower dealing with medico-legal topics.

Electronically Recorded Evidence: A Guide to the Use of Tape and Video Recordings in Criminal and Civil Proceedings
By Sybil Sharpe, 127pp. Fourmat Publishing, £14.95

Electronically recorded evidence is becoming more and more widely used in all fields of law, and particularly in the area of criminal prosecutions and also in cases involving children. Whilst this type of evidence is becoming more familiar, it is also regarded, as is all new development, with suspicion. The courts are slowly becoming easier with the concept of such evidence, and this guide to its use and the legislation currently in force as to its use is very useful indeed. Lawyers, for instance, can read how surveillance equipment may be used, and also how this comes into conflict with the rights and freedom of the individual. The burning question for family law practitioners is that of the use of video links in cases with child witnesses, and the use of video-recorded evidence. This book contains much useful discussion, and is a good addition to the reference shelf.

Child Care and the Courts
By C.R. Smith, M.T. Lane and T. Walsh, Macmillan Education Ltd, £20.00 and £6.95

These three authors have together combined their experience in social work and law to look at the background to care cases. They look at the reasoning of the courts and the social and economic pressures which come into play in child care cases. They discuss common dilemmas, and they take a look at the problems of inter-agency cooperation, or lack of it. They set out briefly the legislative framework and the rules of evidence and trial procedure, offering advice on all sorts of practical topics ranging from how one should present oneself in court to attitudes that can prove helpful or very unhelpful in preparation of cases for court. The authors' obvious practical experience is very valuable, especially for those who may be new to the court scene, and who need an insight into some of the potential problems that might arise on a practical level.

Focus on Child Abuse
Edited by A. Levy, Hawksmere Ltd, 184pp.

This is a collection of chapters by different authors on the subject of child abuse. It has the air of a seminar about it, and in fact stems from a seminar given in Hawksmere in February 1988 chaired by Mr Justice Waterhouse.

The contributors to the book are from different professions, including a solicitor, John Ellison; social worker and guardian *ad litem*, Margaret Adcock; two police officers, Graham Anthony and Anthony Kerr; two paediatricians, Dr Jane Watkeys and Dr Jane Wynne; and a psychiatrist, Dr Stephen Wolkind. This work includes the views of Mr Justice Waterhouse, a High Court judge, and Sean Enright, a barrister. It is useful to see how the judge views some of the issues which cause concern. Jane Jenkins, a child abuse coordinator and Margery Bray, a social work consultant, both add contributions to the book.

There is a chapter on the role of the Official Solicitor, and it is very succinct in its appraisal of the function of this office.

The medical and psychiatric aspects of child abuse are given attention, and there is a discussion of the use of video techniques of interview, anatomically correct dolls, and much more.

The book contains the recommendations of the Cleveland Report 1988 in full, set out in an appendix, and there is a chapter contributed by Alan Levy on the Cleveland Child Abuse Enquiry.

Useful, readable, containing much factual information, and well worth obtaining.

Divorce, Legal Procedures and Financial Facts
Edited by Edith Rudinger, 254pp., Consumers Association, Which Books, £6.95

This is a brilliant little book. It takes a practical approach to the difficulties of working through divorce, and looks at the financial aspects of divorce negotiations. It emphasises that the main part of the problems arising in negotiating through a divorce are caused by lack of honest or effective communication, and that this is essential from the beginning. It is written in a forthright and very straightforward way, aimed at those who are involved in a divorce, or contemplating it. However, practitioners would find it very useful. The facts that are given are useful for those who have to advise on settlements, and the advice offered is not beneath the qualified legal practitioner, and would certainly be very useful for trainees, both in law and in other fields such as social work.

It is good to have a list of the figures used by registrars for reference in calculating maintenance payable for children; foster-parent rates of payment for fostering children; and much more. There is, too, a chart of the divorce procedures, which sets out the flow of proceedings clearly and concisely.

All in all, a very useful reference book, up to date as at April 1989.

Distribution of Matrimonial Assets on Divorce
By Michael L. Rakusen, Dr Peter Hunt and A. Jane Bridge, 3rd Edition, Butterworth & Co., 259pp.

The main difficulty which any practitioner faces when advising clients on divorce and ancillary relief (or ancillary relief in any matrimonial proceedings) is how on earth to make an educated guess at the amount which the court would consider appropriate in the circumstances of the case for maintenance of a former spouse or a child of the family; and also the types of order which the court would consider appropriate in all the circumstances. This book is helpful in providing for reference a good many decided cases, reported in sufficient detail to give the practitioner an idea of the rationale of the courts, and also authorities where required.

There is a comprehensive index.

The book was fully up to date in February 1989, and is a useful work to have for reference.